BERVIE *and* BEYOND

THOM FAMILY HISTORY

To:-
Dad & Mum
lots of love
Tumeewoo x x x

BERVIE *and* BEYOND

THOM FAMILY HISTORY

COLIN W. THOM

COVER PHOTO: THE OLD CHURCHYARD, KIRKBURN, BERVIE

To order additional copies of this book, contact:
Xlibris Corporation
1-800-618-969
www.xlibris.com.au
Orders@xlibris.com.au
502411

CONTENTS

Figures

Credit

The copyrighted map shown as Appendix 1 is used with the kind permission of the owner, Nicolson Maps of Largs, Ayrshire, Scotland, <nicolsonmaps.com>.

INTRODUCTION

My interest in the Thom family history began when my uncle Geoff Thom visited Dublin in the early 1960s. He located his second cousins, Alex and Bolton Thom, and re-established links between the Irish and Australian branches. Family members around the globe had corresponded with each other for many years before that, but most of those links lapsed by the mid-1900s, as the correspondents passed away. Consolidating a family history probably never occurred to any of them at the time . . . more is the pity, as so much knowledge was lost with their demise.

In the late 1970s, I visited Ireland for the first time and met the same Bolton Thom my uncle had met fifteen years earlier. Bolton was an enthusiastic family historian, and some of his enthusiasm rubbed off on to me. When I began my own research, I had a very simple objective: to go back to my earliest traceable paternal ancestor (at the time, my three times great-grandfather, Walter Thom) and then to trace every descendant from him, wherever in the world he or she lived. I recognised it was a very ambitious, but achievable, project. Then I had lapses of inactivity over the next twenty or so years, during which time another generation had come along. But so had the Internet, which made research and communications so much easier.

A visit to Aberdeen, Scotland, in 2008 re-kindled my enthusiasm. I established the identities of Walter's parents and those of his five siblings. And then in 2011, I established the identity of Walter's grandparents. These discoveries magnified my original task more than ten-fold, and clearly, that was beyond me. Therefore, many early sub-branches of the greater family remain either not researched or incomplete, leaving plenty of scope for exploration by others.

In documenting the family tree, it became clear that identification other than by name alone was required to avoid confusion between persons with the same or similar names. Accordingly, each person is assigned an identification number comprising two elements. The 'whole number' digit(s) signifies the generation in which the person belongs, with Generation 1 signifying the earliest traceable generation. The second group of three digits (those after the 'decimal point') signifies the chronological order of birth of that person within that generation, regardless of branch. Hence, the person with identification number 5.015 would be the fifteenth person born in the fifth generation. His or her spouse (or unmarried co-parent) would carry the same basic identification number, plus suffix A, B, or C, depending on whether they were the first, second, or third spouse or co-parent.

To reflect not just bloodlines, but family history as well, adoptees and step-children are included, notated accordingly. Unmarried partners who are co-parents are included, but unmarried partners who are not co-parents are not. Divorces are not recorded. In order to truly reflect the growth in family size over time, the statistics in Appendix 22 include only bloodline descendants.

The family trees contain full name, birth (b) or christening (c) date and place, marriage (m) date and place, date of death (d) and when known, place where buried (b'd), or where died. But the real history and interest is in the text, either extracted from publicly available documents or supplied from within the family. The text concentrates on the lives of those in Generations 2 to 7 but extends into later generations when a particular person has achieved something especially worthwhile that is recognised in the broader community.

Many Generation 8 family members are in their twilight years; I urge them to record their own sub-branch history for the benefit of their immediate descendants and those yet to come before that history is lost forever. Further, blank pages are included at the back of the book for recording the arrival of new family members, as was the practice with the old family Bible in the past.

Deciding the book title was a simple task. The family originated in the parish of Bervie in Scotland, and its members have dispersed all over the globe—to Ireland, England, Argentina, USA, Africa, France, and Australia, to name but a few. But wherever we are and whatever our family name, we still have one thing in common: we all share the blood of the 'original' Alexander Thom, born 1715.

This book would not have been possible without the encouragement, support, and generous hospitality of many.

Bolton Thom and his daughters Margaret, Barbara, Rosemary, and Hilary deserve special mention in this regard. Sally Henderson was a prolific writer, and her stories add interest. Even though she didn't know it at the time, she did us all a great favour in having her father, Alexander, record his life experiences so many years ago. Harry Thom and his sister Pat Sword in Argentina were both helpful with input and generous with hospitality during my visit there. Lorraine Hornidge helped open up to me the mystery of the Pilkington branch. My many Australian relatives assisted with data on their families which I could not have obtained otherwise; Beverley Wain in particular has been most helpful with research and supplying family data. Of those outside of the family, I am most indebted to Isles Burness of Bervie, Frances Wilkins of Aberdeen, Jimmie Robinson and Maria Wootton, both of Dublin, and Cecil Potterton of Kildare. To all of the above and others not mentioned here, I offer my thanks for your assistance.

And a special thank you to my wife, Shirley, for doing things around the home that I should have been doing, whilst I thumped away on the keyboard in the study.

Colin W Thom
Southport, Queensland, Australia
6 October 2012

CHAPTER 1

THE ALEXANDERS OF SCOTLAND

The earliest verified record of our Thom forebears is the marriage of Alexander Thom (id. 1.001) and Margaret Dorward (id. 1.001A) on 14 September 1732 in the parish of Kinneff and Catterline in Kincardineshire, Scotland. Alexander had been born in Bervie in 1715 and was only seventeen years of age. Margaret had been born just three miles away in Kinneff in 1718 and was only fourteen years old.

Nothing is known of the parents of either Alexander or Margaret, as records for the public at large prior to the early 1700s are quite rare. However, we do know that in those times, families tended to remain in the one district for generations, and it is more than likely those parents were born and lived their whole lives in Kincardineshire. We also know that often for economic reasons, not all children were christened.

Kincardineshire, also known as The Mearns, was described in records of the day as a maritime county on the north-east coast of Scotland. It was bounded on the north by Aberdeenshire, from which it was partly separated by the River Dee. To the south and west, the North Esk River, in part, separated it from Forfar County. Kincardineshire had a total area of 382 square miles, almost equally divided between cultivated and virgin land. The shire's name comes from Kincardine, formerly a small town in the parish of Fordoun, which was the seat of the county court until the year 1600, when it was transferred to Stonehaven, located on the coast midway between Aberdeen City and Montrose. The parish of Bervie (also known as the parish of Inverbervie) was named because of the Bervie River on its north-eastern boundary. Bervie is an ancient English word signifying a boiling or ebullition and is descriptive of the peculiar course of the water. The township of Inverbervie is at the mouth of the River Bervie. Its most famous son is Hercules Linton, who built the tea clipper, the *Cutty Sark*. A farming community about eight miles inland named Glenbervie is best known for its cemetery, which is the burial site of the parents of Scottish poet Robbie Burns. Kincardineshire is now incorporated into Aberdeenshire. A modern map of the area is shown as Appendix 1.

Alexander and Margaret had two children: Anne (id. 2.001) was christened on 6 March 1738 in the parish of Kinneff and Catterline; Alexander (id. 2.002) was born four years later in the same parish. His christening was recorded as below:

> 1742. January 3. Alexander Thom and Margaret Dorward in Middletown of Barras had a child baptized Alexander.

We all are the descendants of this second Alexander. Nothing is known of his childhood or early adult life, but it is reasonable to assume he remained a resident of Kincardineshire; nor is anything known of his sister Anne, and research on her is beyond the scope of this family history. The date of death and burial place for their parents are not known; Bervie is the most likely location.

In 1763, having just reached the age of majority, Alexander married. Records state:

> Alexander Thom Merchant in Bervie and Christian Henderson in this Parish formerly contracted and lawfully proclaimed were married upon Saturday June the fourth day.

Alexander and Christian had six children over the following nine years. A daughter, Christian (id. 3.001), was born in 1764; Alexander (id. 3.002) in 1766; John (id. 3.003) in 1767; James (id. 3.004) in 1768; Walter (id. 3.005) in 1770, and Jean (id. 3.006) in 1773. We all are the descendants of Walter. The family tree for these early generations is shown as Appendix 15. The writer has not traced the lives or families of Walter's five siblings; for practical reasons, that task also is deemed outside the scope of this particular family history. Nonetheless, to assist future researchers, it should be noted Kincardineshire records show that:

> Christian Thom married Alexander Thom at Glenbervie on 16 March 1788, or possibly at Bervie on 24 March 1788.

> John Thom married Margaret Walker at Dunnottar on 17 January 1795.

> James Thom married Elisabeth Robertson at Bervie on 26 March 1785.

> James Thom married Jean Lamb at Dunnottar on 22 December 1787.

James Thom married Elspet Grant at Dunnottar on 17 January 1795.

Jean Thom married Patrick Rolland at Bervie on 20 August 1794.

No claim or otherwise is made that any of the above were siblings of Walter, but the possibility remains that they might have been.

Alexander the Smuggler

As indicated in his marriage record, Alexander was a merchant, but of what is not known. According to local Bervie historian Isles J Burness, Alexander was listed on the 1771 Cess Roll with an assessed mercantile trade of £100. This apparently was insufficient to provide for a growing family, so he turned his entrepreneurial skills to a more lucrative, if questionable, discipline. The *Smuggling Story of the Northern Shores (Oban to Montrose, including the Islands)*, by Frances Wilkins, published in 1995, states:

In early December 1773, the collector described Alexander Thom as 'a smuggler of inferior note with respect to Sime, though I am credibly informed that he presently is in good circumstances.' On 28 December 1773, William Blews seized fifteen casks of tea (1071 lbs sound and 13 lbs damaged), four ankers of Geneva (34 gallons), and one matt of tobacco (44 lbs leaf tobacco) together with an open boat which had been used in running the goods ashore, lying at the Burn of Benholm. The smuggle had been carried on by Alexander Thom, who, after the goods were landed among the rocks where they were found by Blews, went in the boat to board the vessel and sailed to Auchmithie, where the rest of the cargo was smuggled. This vessel was a pink-sterned sloop, the sole property of Walter Sime. In June 1774, Blews identified her as the *Katherine* of Johnshaven, Alexander Law master, but he had not been able to seize her. When the seized tea was put up for sale at Montrose, nobody came to purchase; the collector believed this was because Sime had made an agreement with the local merchants about it. The tea was sent to Leith to be sold.

In 1775, Alexander Thom was prosecuted for the sum of £1650, being treble the value of goods: one hundred and twenty-six ankers Geneva, twenty-six matts tobacco, and eighty matts tobacco stalks, which he assisted in unshipping. The prosecution was based on the information of William Blews relating to a run at land of Shield Hill in February 1772. Thom hired boats from Shield Hill to take the goods. They went out to the ship, the *Ann*, loaded the goods but could not return to the shore because of the high seas. As a result, Thom ordered the goods on board again, except for the loading of one boat, which overset. He then went with the vessel to Johnshaven, where another boat made three trips to unload the goods. Thom went ashore with the third load.

In October 1775, Thom submitted a petition to the Board. He wanted the trial postponed because several of the material witnesses were overseas. 'The petitioner has also the misfortune of being in very low circumstances in life. He has a wife and a numerous family of young children for whose subsistence it is with the utmost difficulty he can provide. In that situation he can ill afford the charge of defending himself against a prosecution of this nature, although in the issue he is humbly confident of success. He is therefore advised to make this application to Your Honours in hopes that you will accept from him the sum of £70, with such costs as have been already incurred, being the utmost that he can raise by the assistance of his friends for as he has already said his own funds can afford nothing.' The board agreed to accept £85.

Alexander the Linen Weaver

In 1777, Alexander joined forces with his friend Sime to form the company of Sime and Thom, set up to manufacture thread. In 1787, it was granted a licence by Kendrew and Porthouse of Darlington to erect a machine for spinning linen yarn. The book *Reminiscences of Flax Spinning* by William Brown, Dundee 1862 states:

Commencement in Scotland: Mill at Bervie

In this country flax-spinning by machinery was early commenced. In 1787, the year in which the patent was granted to Kendrew and Porthouse, a mill was erected, considered to be the first of its kind in Scotland, situate at Bervie, in Kincardineshire, on the stream there, called the water of Bervie. As some proof of its having been the first, it is stated in Leigh's *Road Book of Scotland*, that the town of Bervie presents two things to the notice of travellers; a small harbour for fishing boats, and a machine for spinning linen yarn, said to be the first of its kind in Scotland. No date is given. Another proof to same point is that, long afterwards, on part of the original machinery being taken down for improvement, there was found within the driving drum, an inscription of date 1787, written by one of the mechanics who first fitted up the machinery, stating the work to have been erected in the above year: also some lines as to the nature of it, and the offence given the hand-spinners of Bervie, whose living was endangered thereby; and whose rage consequently was bitter against all concerned in the erection.

Further proof: In Sir John Sinclair's *Statistical Account of Scotland*, it is stated, under title Parish of Bervie, written by Mr Walter Thom, 'Three years ago, a machine was erected on the haughs of Bervie for spinning linen yarn, being the first of its kind in Scotland.' No date was given for this information, but as Sir John's queries were circulated throughout Scotland early in 1790, if Mr Thom had replied to the same in that year, it would bring the date of the erection of the mill to 1787. The work was got up at first by Mr Thom and, some say, one or two others on a ground lease of ninety-nine years. The machinery was procured from England through the patentees of Darlington, who also personally advised regarding erection generally. The extent at first was eight frames or sides of 24 spindles each, being 192 spindles in all, adapted for spinning flax. The building was in size equal to many more. No tows were as yet spun by machinery. At present day, the extent of the work is three or four times the above, with steam power in addition to the running stream. The work has moved on pretty steadily from the beginning under various owners. At the age now of seventy-five years, it can look back upon hundreds of others—its followers—who have pursued the same object, though with success exceedingly various as amongst themselves. Some have failed altogether and disappeared—some have merely kept moving on, bordering on failure—others have yielded fair returns in their way—and a few attained high fame and fortune. Should this work at Bervie continue spinning for a similar length of time, it will likely have better things to look back upon amongst its followers—mills more steady in their career and success: their internal arrangements more simple and commodious, with their sanitary condition and educational matters standing high.

Walter Thom in the above-mentioned 1790 report also stated:

Although exceedingly imperfect at first, it is now brought to a considerable degree of improvement; the yarn it spins is of a good quality, and fit for any sort of manufacture whatever. The proprietors of the machine have also the thread manufacture, so that all the yarn spun by the machine is made into threads. The house is not yet filled with machinery, but will contain from 600 to 700 spindles when full, and employ about sixty boys and girls and twenty or thirty men and women.

Records held by Burness show the value of the Sime and Thom business was assessed at £400 in 1790 and £1000 the following year, which suggests the teething troubles mentioned in the statistical account had been overcome and the output of yarn greatly increased. The partnership continued until 1803, about which time Alexander died. His wife took over the business in 1806 and changed the name to Mrs Alex Thom and Co. The final entry for the firm was in 1809, when business was assessed at £100 of trade. The date of death and burial site for both Alexander and Christian are not known.

The Old Linen Mill 2008

In May 2008, the writer visited the Aberdeen region to research the family history. Inverbervie is about thirty kilometres south of Aberdeen, just beyond Stonehaven. A road sign 'The Haughs of Bervie (Industrial Estate)' was the vital clue which led me to the old linen mill. At the end of a road running alongside the river was an industrial complex, a mix of old buildings and more recent structures, operating as a warehouse for Oil Technics Ltd, a fire-fighting foam supplier to the North Sea oil rigs off Aberdeen.

Current owner David Evans confirmed the old building within his complex was the first linen mill in Scotland, and the title deeds verify the original owner was our Alexander. The building viewed from the south-east is shown as Figure 1.

Figure 1: Linen Mill

The paddle wheel which powered the machinery for making linen thread no longer exists, but the concrete base for it remains. A man-made canal which diverted water from the Bervie to the paddle wheel is still evident; sluice gates at the entrance to the canal controlled the flow. The walls and roof of the building are intact, as is the roof frame, made from tree trunks. Evans intends to relocate his commercial activities from the site in the near future and establish residential quarters in the old mill. The official postal address is Upper Mill, Inverbervie, Aberdeenshire. It is readily visible on Google Earth at coordinates 56 degrees, 51 minutes,

06.37 seconds north, and 02 degrees, 17 minutes, 26.24 seconds west. It is distinguishable from the remainder of the complex by its north-south pitched roof ridge. Located on the same property about 100 m to the east is a late eighteenth-century home in which Alexander and family lived and which is now the Evans' family home (see Figure 2). The remains of a second smaller linen mill are evident at the bottom of the garden.

Figure 2: Family Home Inverbervie

CHAPTER 2

WALTER OF SCOTLAND AND IRELAND

Walter (id. 3.005) was born in Bervie, Kincardineshire, on 14 April 1770, the fifth child of Alexander and Christian. Church records of his christening state:

> Thom Walter lawfull Son to Alexander Thom Merchant in Bervie and Christian Henderson his Spouse was baptized upon Wednesday April the eighteenth day before sundry witnesses.

Walter grew up in the area, but little else is known of his childhood. As noted by Dublin-based writer Maria Wootton:

It would appear that Walter saw very little future in weaving at Bervie, or perhaps, being the fifth born, there was no room for him in the family business, and so he moved to Aberdeen and set himself up as a bookseller. He acquired some reputation as a writer on historical and statistical matters.

The Statistical Account of Scotland 1791-9

In introducing the 1982 edition of this tome, the editor noted:

The Statistical Account of Scotland has been used for generation after generation of social historians enquiring into the local or national affairs of Scotland in the late eighteenth century. It is an unrivalled source, and historians of other countries, as well as their sociologists, geographers and natural scientists, have long regretted having no similar body of evidence available to them. Sir John Sinclair, determinedly cajoling the parish ministers of the Established Church to respond to his long list of over 160 queries, intended his statistical enquiry to enable the country, and its government, not only to assess its current state but to prepare better for a better future.

It is unclear how or why Walter Thom became responsible for reporting on the parish of Inverbervie or Bervie (further proof of the flexibility of names) rather than the parish minister, but the success of his efforts determined his life path. Some interesting facts Walter included in his report are listed below:

The parish population was 985, with 607 in Bervie, 188 in Gourdon, and 190 in the rural areas of the parish. Bervie consisted of three streets which formed three sides of a square with 110 houses.

The main legal trade was fishing, particularly for salmon, but Bervie also was famous, or infamous, for an illicit and illegal trade in teas, spirits, and tobacco. From 1750, sail-cloth manufacture was established in Montrose, and from it grew the weaving industry. Walter then went on to describe the establishment of the first linen mill at Bervie but did not mention that his father was behind this venture.

There were nine shops in Bervie, selling soft ware, grocery goods etc. There were five ale houses and a tavern intended principally for accommodation.

The church was built in 1781. The poor were about twelve in general. They received about £28 a year, divided among them, 'which arises from the interest of some money lent out, and the weekly collections at the church door'.

A ploughman capable of sowing received from £3 to £10 yearly, and his victuals; a maid servant from £5 to £6; a boy from £2 to £3; a day labourer one shilling a day; a mason 1s 8d a day; a joiner 1s 1d, and a tailor 8d a day, and victuals.

The parish area was 1660 Scot acres or 2399 English acres. About half of it was arable. Farmland was owned by only Viscount Arbuthnot and Mr Barklay of Ury. There were sixteen ploughs, sixty-one horses, and some oxen used in farming.

There once existed in Bervie a religious order of white friars, 'but nothing now remains'.

The inhabitants of Bervie had contracted with a man to bring in water to the town by pipes. The sum necessary to defray the expense was to be raised by a tax of one shilling on each hearth.

A copy of the 1791-9 study edited by Sir John Sinclair is held in the Thom Bequest in the National Library of Ireland. The leading pages of Walter's twelve-page contribution to Sinclair's publication are shown as Appendix 2.

The History of Aberdeen

This two-volume book was published in 1811 and arguably was Walter's most famous work. Its title page describes it as containing an account of the rise, progress, and extension of the city from a remote period to the present day; including its antiquities, civil, and ecclesiastical state; manufactures, trade, and commerce; an account of the See of Aberdeen and the two universities; biographical sketches of eminent men connected with the bishopric and colleges.

The book was printed in Aberdeen by D. Chalmers and Co., for Alex Stevenson, Bookseller, Castle Street and sold by him and all the other booksellers. The title page describes Walter Thom as author of *Sketches on Political Economy,* and other books.

Of possible interest to family members is the story of Bessie Thom, together with two other women, being burnt at the stake in 1596 for witchcraft. Note that Walter neither claimed nor refuted that he and Bessie were related. Volume 1, Page 270 states:

During this and the following year, no fewer than twenty-three persons lost their lives for the crime of witchcraft, of whom one died in prison, another hanged herself, and twenty-one suffered at the stake. An account of the expence of their execution is recorded; and as a specimen of the price and quantity of the materials used for burning witches, the following is presented, viz.

Christine Mitchell, Bessie Thom, and Isobel Barrow 5 March, 1596.

Item, For a boll and a half of coals to burn the said witches, 50 shillings.

Item, For thirty-five loads of peats, £4 10s.

Item, For six barrels of tar, £10.1s.

Item, For two iron barrels, eight shillings.

Item, For a stake, dressing and setting up, 13s. 8d.

Item, For eight fathoms of rope, eight shillings.

Item, For the carrying of the coals, peats and barrels, eight shillings.

Item, To John Justice (the hangman) for his fee, 20 shillings.

The poor people were accused of being the d—l's agents; and it is astonishing that the reformed clergy could have believed that his sable majesty, to whom they ascribed so much cunning, should have employed only ignorant, old, and decrepit women as his instruments in carrying on his war against mankind. (Writer's Note. It was considered inappropriate at the time to express the term 'devil').

A copy of *The History of Aberdeen* is held in the Thom Collection at the National Library of Ireland. This writer purchased a copy in 2008 from an Aberdeen book seller for £150. A family copy is held by Barbara Barrett (nee Thom) of New Ross, Eire. The title page is shown as Appendix 3. Reprints of both volumes of the book have been available since 2009. Electronic versions also are available for purchase, but the full text also can be read online at no cost.

Pedestrianism

This book was published 1 January 1813. It is attributed to the author of *The History of Aberdeen*, but it is not until the end of the preface that Walter's name appears. Printing was by D. Chalmers and Co., Aberdeen. The title page describes the book as an account of the performances of celebrated pedestrians during the eighteenth and early nineteenth centuries, with a full narrative of Captain Barclay's public and private matches and an essay on training. Noted reviewer J. K. Gillon summarised the book as follows:

The Celebrated Pedestrian

Robert Barclay Allardice, who was universally known as Captain Barclay, was born in August 1777 at Ury House just outside Stonehaven in Scotland. Barclay was one of the strongest men of his time, which seems to have been a family trait. His family were famous for their muscular prowess, and pastimes such as wrestling bulls, carrying sacks of flour in their teeth and uprooting trees with their bare hands were part of the Barclay tradition. As a boy, Barclay played with a two-handed sword which was too heavy for most grown men to lift. By the age of twenty he could lift an eighteen stone man from the floor to a table with one hand. Hammer throwing and caber tossing were like children's games to Barclay.

However it was his extraordinary walking feats that earned Barclay his greatest renown and the title of the 'Celebrated Pedestrian'. Long distance walking was a popular spectator sport in the eighteenth and nineteenth centuries with huge crowds willing to pay entrance fees to watch walking events. It could also be extremely lucrative for its top competitors, particularly if, like Barclay, they were not adverse to a degree of gamesmanship to stack up the odds. In 1801, he wagered a thousand guineas that he could walk 90 miles in twenty-one hours, but reputedly caught a cold, and lost. He then increased the stake to 2,000 guineas, and lost again. He then got odds which would pay him 5,000 guineas if he won, which he did, with an hour to spare.

His first recorded competitive walking performance was in 1796 when he walked for 110 miles in 19 hours twenty-seven minutes in a muddy park; in the same year he did 90 miles in twenty hours two minutes; in 1802 he went 64 miles in ten hours; in 1805 he walked 72 miles between breakfast and dinner; in 1806 he walked 110 miles 100 miles over bad roads in nineteen hours; and in 1807, 78 miles on hilly roads in fourteen hours. In 1808, he started at 5 a.m., walked 30 miles grouse shooting, walked 60 miles home in eleven hours, dined and walked 16 miles to a ball, returned to his home by 7 a.m., and spent the next day shooting, having travelled 130 miles and gone without sleep for two nights.

In 1809, at Newmarket he accomplished his most noted feat of endurance walking. This involved walking one mile in each of 1000 successive hours. In other words Barclay was required to walk a mile an hour, every hour, for forty two days and nights. Barclay started on 1 June and completed his historic feat on 12 July. His average time varied from fourteen minutes fifty-four seconds in the first week to twenty-one minutes four seconds in the last week. Over 10,000 people were attracted to the event and Barclay picked up substantial prize money for his efforts.

Walter Thom in his book *Pedestrianism*, published in 1813, describes Captain Barclay's 'astonishing exploits', provides a table of his pedestrian activities, a journal of his Newmarket walk, and a chapter on his genealogy and family history. Barclay himself provides a chapter on his training methods. It seems, however, that he did not adhere strictly to any rigorous training regime and had a reputation for hearty eating and drinking. Despite this, Barclay had a profound impact on athletics generally, and his training methods, involving purging and sweating and the eating of meat, were widely used throughout much of the century.

Barclay also eschewed any form of athletic strip, and his preferred form of dress for competition consisted of a top hat, cravat, warm woollen suit, lambs wool socks, and thick-soled shoes. Walter Thom attributes Captain Barclay's pedestrian powers to his great strength and his walking style that involved bending the body forward to throw the weight on his knees, taking short steps, and raising his feet only a few inches from the ground.

Captan Barclay's other main sporting interest was boxing, in which he acted as sponsor and trainer of Tom Cribb, the bare knuckles Champion of the World in 1807 and 1809. He was also a distinguished soldier, an excellent shot, and a successful gambler. In his fifties, Barclay started a new business venture: the Defiance stagecoach that ran between Aberdeen and Glasgow. Barclay made the Defiance one of the most efficient and reliable stagecoach services that Scotland had ever seen. Despite his predilection for pedestrianism, Barclay was an accomplished stagecoach driver and is credited with taking the London mail coach to Aberdeen single-handed, which required him to be in the driver's seat for nearly three days and nights. Captain Barclay met his end on 8 May 1854, dying of paralysis a few days after being kicked by a horse.

Readers might think this all very interesting, but apart from writing the book on Barclay, of what relevance is that to Walter Thom? It had always intrigued the writer that Walter's books and articles on statistical, historic, and/or economic matters were always of a serious nature, whilst *Pedestrianism* was essentially a biography of a sporting hero. It appeared to be out of character for him. But a casual comment by David Evans, current owner of the old linen mill, as he walked me around the site changed all that. He commented that Castle Allardice, a sixteenth-century manor house just up the river was the ancestral home of the captain's mother, Sarah Allardice. Captain Barclay and his father farmed the land around Castle Allardice, and it is possible that Walter Thom knew the captain from childhood, despite a seven-year age difference. In the preface to his book, Walter states that he undertook to write it at the suggestion of a few friends, which might have included Barclay himself or local citizens who saw the merits of recording for posterity the feats of this local identity. Barclay himself contributed the chapter on training and is said to have overseen the other chapters of the book.

A copy is held in the Thom Collection at the National Library of Ireland; its title page is shown as Appendix 4. In 2008, the writer purchased a copy in London for £380. The only other copy available at the time was for sale at US $1200. Paperback reprints of the book are now available.

Other Publications

Sketches on Political Economy, mentioned on the title page of *The History of Aberdeen* as another of Walter's books, was published in 1809. There is no copy of it in the Thom Collection at the National Library of Ireland, nor is it listed in the Goldsmith's-Kress Library of Economic Literature, which combines the resources of the Goldsmith's Library of Economic Literature at the University of London and the Kress Library of Business and Economics at Harvard Graduate School of Business Administration at Boston, Massachusetts, USA. However, Goldsmith's-Kress does attribute another publication titled *Synopsis of the Science of Political Economy* to Walter. It was published in 1814 in Dublin, by which time he had taken up residence there. No copy exists in the Thom Collection, but an original example of the thirty-two-page book is held in the USA, and microfilm copies are held at five universities around Australia (Reference GK # 20897). The title page is shown as Appendix 5.

Given Walter's literary efforts over most of his life, it is not surprising that he is referred to in Cates' *Dictionary of General Biography* as being a noted writer, poet, and statistician.

Marriage and Family

In 1800, one day short of his thirtieth birthday, Walter married Margaret Turner, the fourth daughter of John Turner Esq. of Ellon, Aberdeenshire. Turner Hall, the family home, is shown as Figure 3. We can reasonably assume Walter married well; the 1845 edition of *The New Statistical Account of Scotland*, Volume XII, Aberdeen, Parish of Ellon states:

Figure 3: Turner Hall

Turner Hall, the seat of the Turner family, is situated about two miles north from the village of Ellon, on the acclivity of an elevation whose summit is probably the highest ground in the whole parish. It commands a most extensive prospect, comprehending a long range of the German Ocean, the higher grounds in the vicinity of Aberdeen, many of the Donside, Deeside, and several also of the Speyside mountains, together with an immense stretch of the intervening country. The house is of an inferior description, patched-like in its appearance, and extremely limited in point of accommodation. The locality is not particularly favourable, but much has been done of late years to improve the grounds; and the circumstance that there are a few tolerably good trees in the lawn forbids peremptorily a change of site.

There are eight proprietors of land in the parish, each of whom draws an annual income from it of upwards of £50. John Turner of Turner Hall . . . Estate 1956 Scotch acres, of which 1450 were arable.

Walter and Margaret had four children: Alexander (id. 4.001) born April 18, 1801; Elizabeth Helen (id. 4.002) in 1802; another Elizabeth Helen (id. 4.003) in 1804, and Jean (id. 4.004), in 1806. See Appendix 15. The two girls named Elizabeth Helen died in infancy, and Jean died unmarried and childless in 1832; it is not known where she was buried. We all are descendants of Alexander.

Career

As a young man, Walter became a merchant in Bervie, though of what is not known. Probably because of the success of his report on the parish of Bervie for *The Statistical Account of Scotland*, he saw a better future as a writer and moved to Aberdeen to continue his chosen occupation, complemented by his book-selling business. According to the *Aberdeen Journal* of 30 June, 1824, following his death, Walter lived in Aberdeen for only three years (probably circa 1809 to 1812) before moving to Edinburgh to concentrate fully on his writing. This correlates with the obituary of his son Alexander, who attended Edinburgh High School.

In 1813, Robert Peel, Chief Secretary of Ireland, invited Walter to move to its capital and edit Faulkner's *Dublin Journal*, a government-subsidised evening newspaper issued each Monday, Wednesday, and Friday at five pence a copy, published and printed at 15 Parliament Street near City Hall. The newspaper's editorial comment strongly reflected the government position on policy matters. Walter accepted the offer and moved to Dublin, where he lived above the premises.

In 1819, Robert Peel retired and handed over the proprietorship of the newspaper to Walter. Around this time, Walter became a founding member of the local Association for the Suppression of Mendacity. He also contributed to *Brewster's Encyclopaedia* and to Mason's *Statistical Account of Ireland*.

Up until 1820, things went fairly well with the *Dublin Journal*, but then prospects for the paper were seriously affected by changes in imperial policy towards Ireland, brought about by the appointment of the Marquis of Wellesley as Lord Lieutenant. He supported Catholic emancipation, which conflicted with the views expressed in Walter's newspaper. Its editorial policy became unacceptable to some of its Irish Protestant readers, who switched to the recently introduced *Evening Mail*, and circulation reduced to about 300 copies per issue. Despite it being unprofitable, Walter struggled on with the *Dublin Journal*, but the stress took its toll on him. He died at the age of fifty-four, on 16 June 1824. He was buried at St Luke's Church, The Coombe, Dublin. His wife, Margaret, was buried alongside him eighteen years later. Their son Alex later in his life erected a tablet in the church, commemorating them.

Other Thom Scribes from Scotland

Walter was not the only Thom in Scotland handy with pen and paper. William Thom, commonly referred to as the Inverurie Poet, in 1844 released *The Rhymes and Recollections of a Hand-Loom Weaver*. He was born in Aberdeen in 1798, the son of shopkeeper John Thom, who died during William's infancy. He was put to work at the age of ten in a cotton mill and had a hard life. He became an itinerant musician and poet, but it was not until late in life that he achieved widespread recognition with his *Recollections* book. He died in 1848. Given that his Aberdeen birthplace was not far removed from Kincardineshire, William may have been related to Walter, though no claim or otherwise is made in this regard. Nonetheless, it is worthy of mention that a copy of William's 1844 book held by Margaret Denton (nee Thom) of Sissinghurst, Kent, has inscribed in its front pages: 'Willie joins me in regards to all. Yours very truly, Mr Thom, June 1845'.

Another William Thom, 1710-90, from Glasgow, issued books in 1762 and 1771, and Reverend William Thom, A. M. Minister of Govan, issued a book in 1782, also in Glasgow. It is believed neither of these authors was directly linked to our branch.

CHAPTER 3

ALEXANDER OF IRELAND

Alex the Printer Publisher

It is uncertain when Alex moved from Scotland to Ireland. Various reference sources including the *Oxford Dictionary of National Biography* suggest it was not until 1820, when Alex gave up his studies at Edinburgh High School and moved to Dublin to assist his father, whose newspaper had fallen on hard times. Other references suggest Alex moved to Ireland either with his father in 1813 or not long after, but certainly in his teenage years. In an article in the *Dublin Historical Record* of March-May 1946, author Joseph W. Hammond wrote:

Mr Carse, the present editor of Thom's Directory, tells me that he can recall Mr Thom himself stating that he wrote out a manuscript poster announcing the victory of Waterloo in 1815 and pasted it on the wall of his father's house in Parliament Street . . . The belief that young Alexander Thom was brought over to Dublin long before 1820 receives some support from the fact that the 'Report of the Association for the Suppression of Mendacity in Dublin for the Year 1818'—a forty-eight page crown octavo pamphlet in my possession—bears the following imprint: 'Dublin: Printed by A. Thom, 15 Parliament Street. 1819.' This is probably the earliest imprint bearing the name of A. Thom, and it seems to me that his father did that to encourage young Alexander in his career as a printer and publisher.

Work in the printing trade then was vastly different from today's conditions, and Thom's was typical of the industry. Men worked from seven in the morning to seven in the evening and rarely grumbled, because they regarded labour as a divine ordinance—to earn their bread by the sweat of their brow. The day's work began with the oldest compositor leading his fellow workers in prayer—thanks to Almighty God for having spared them all to see another day, and another prayer for the welfare of their employer for providing them with a job. They worked about sixty-five hours per week, earning about £1.10s on piece-work.

Apprentices had a particularly hard life. Boys began their careers as printers at eleven years of age and worked the same hours as the men. In their first year, they received three shillings per week. In each of the next six years, they received a raise of one shilling, and an exceptionally brilliant apprentice might receive eleven or twelve shillings in his final year of training. These rates of wages might have been temporarily reduced if the lads were heard to curse or swear or found to smoke, play cards, frequent taverns or playhouses, or be seen in bad company; and if a sixth or seventh-year apprentice contracted holy matrimony, his indentures were cancelled and he lost his job. The indenture of the last bound apprentice, who happened to remain with the company for sixty-one years, is shown as Appendix 6.

Alex, like all other employers of his period, disliked trade unionism 'and the perpetual menace of illegal combination', as he is said to have termed it. But he paid his key men extra money, and his chief compositor held the highest-paid position in the Irish printing trade at six guineas a week.

Being the son of the proprietor, Alex of course did not have to endure the rigours of a formal apprenticeship; nonetheless, he had an extensive period of learning the trade and the business. Maria Wootton summarises the early career of Alex as follows:

Alex started to learn the art of printing and publishing with Walter, at the Dublin Journal. Following his father's death, and with declining sales, Alex closed down the Dublin Journal on 8 April 1825, and disposed of the Parliament Street premises. He relocated the printing plant to 139 Mecklenburgh Street (now Waterford Street) on the north side of the city, where he re-started as a general printer in partnership with his foreman, a Mr Johnston, who continued on with teaching him the art and craft of printing. After three years, Alex moved to 21 North Earl Street, where he set himself up as a printer, stationer and bookseller. Business was slow so he decided to apply to Sir Robert Peel, then in London, for some recognition of his and his late father's losses sustained in support of Government policy, which had led to the collapse of the Dublin Journal. Through Peel's influence, the London Stationery Office gave him probably more than he expected—the entire contract for the Post Office printing in Ireland. This included the Post Office

Directory, a competitor to Wilson's Dublin Directory that ceased publication in 1837. He borrowed capital from a friend to enable him to execute this contract, which he did to the satisfaction of the Government, and from then onwards began to prosper. In 1838, he approached Chief Secretary Thomas Drummond, another Scotsman who had adopted Ireland as his home, and managed to secure the printing of all future Royal Commissions in Ireland; this included *Griffith's Primary Valuation of Ireland*, familiar to all genealogists and family history researchers.

The firm of Alex Thom and Co. was now expanding at such a rate that another move to larger premises was necessary. Later that year, Alex transferred his plant to the four-storied premises at 87-88 Middle Abbey Street (now the headquarters of Independent Newspapers), with ground extending back to Prince's Street. The firm continued to expand and prosper; it became the industry leader in the printing trade in Ireland and was the only printing house in Dublin operating its own type foundry.

Nonetheless, it was not all smooth sailing. According to local researchers Georgina Clinton and Sinead Sturgeon:

Thom's business suffered in the economic depression which afflicted the Dublin printing trade from 1839 to 1842. To protect it he attempted to impose stringent working conditions on his employees (an eleven hour working day and binding one year contracts). This provoked a widespread strike among his employees, and the Dublin Typographical Provident Society banned its members from working in his office.

But the business survived and indeed continued to prosper. Alex's success was not achieved by good fortune; he was dedicated to the job and to the company, and he knew the trade. The following pen picture of Alex at work is taken from *Progress in Irish Printing* published by Alex Thom and Co. in 1936, well after the demise of its founder.

There he took personal interest, even in the most-minute piece of activity in the factory. Every day, he inspected the work; and each worker waited, not in fear, (but) for the judgements of that low-sized stout man who stood beside them—his be-tasselled velvet smoking cap half-hiding his curly white head and his small hairy hands giving that necessary touch of approval to some form of type. So he went on his daily round, whistling happily as he went among those old gentlemen compositors of his, who came to work dressed in tall hats, frock coats, and carrying umbrellas.

In the 1840s, Alex's eldest daughter, Margaret, married Frederick Pilkington, the government bookbinder whose premises adjoined Thom's. It was only a matter of time before the two firms merged and Frederick began to assume a role in the management of the consolidated company. During this period, Alex launched what was to become the highly successful *Thom's Directory*, about which there will be more later. In 1851, Alex took over the printing and publication of the *Dublin Gazette*. In 1856, a new font was developed by George Petrie, an employee of Alex Thom and Co. It is classified as a Gaelic Modern Round font and is identified by alternative titles Petrie C. and Thom. Petrie previously had developed two other fonts when working for others. The site <evertype.com/celtscript/fonthist.hmtl> provides additional detail.

In 1860, Alex published at his own expense for gratuitous distribution *A Collection of Tracts and Treatises* illustrative of the natural history, antiquities, and the political and social state of Ireland at various periods prior to the present century, two volumes which contain reprints of the works of Ware, Spenser, Sir John Davis, Sir William Petty, Bishop Berkeley, and other writers on Irish affairs.

On 18 February 1870, Alex deviated from his normal position of shunning public office and its attendant public exposure, and accepted an appointment as a Commissioner of the Peace in the borough of Dublin. Compared with a modern day Justice of the Peace (J.P.) whose prime responsibility seems to be certifying copies of legal documents, the role of a Commissioner in the 1870s was much more significant. The duties and authority of Alex and his fellow Commissioners are spelt out in a wordy proclamation handwritten on pigskin accompanying Alex's appointment, and now in the custody of Margaret Denton. The full text is included as Appendix 7.

On 23 March 1876, Alex was appointed the Queen's Printer in Ireland. The appointment (or patent), handwritten on pigskin, also is held by Margaret Denton. Together with The Queen's Seal, it is shown as Figure 4. The full text of the appointment is included as Appendix 8.

Figure 4: Queen's Printer Appointment

In 1877, Alex passed the *Irish Almanac and Directory* business to Frederick Pilkington, and not long after, he appointed journalist Edward Thomas Lefroy to manage the printing business, thus enabling Alex to semi-retire. Lefroy's appointment was a disaster for all parties concerned. After decades of industrial harmony, labour troubles again arose at the company, with the workers seeking a wage rise of two shillings a week. Lefroy dismissed competent craftsmen and brought in inexperienced strike breakers, whose incompetence disorganised what had been an efficient plant. The 26 October 1878 edition of *The Citizen and Irish Artisan* summarised the mood of the day:

A criminal libel suit by Lefroy (is one thing); but a bigger issue is deprivation of work for hundreds of printers and replacement by ruffians at lesser wages.

Alex promptly dismissed Lefroy, but the damage had been done. Lefroy, who had been a close friend of Alex and from March 1878 a trustee, executor, and beneficiary of his will, died within months. It is understood that about this time, Alex was appointed as a magistrate in the courts of Dublin, the duties and mental stress of which would have been somewhat of a burden to a man of his age.

In 1879, after almost six decades in the printing trade, Alex transferred ownership of the company to Frederick Pilkington. He had fretted over its recent instability, and the stress is said to have contributed to his death not long after.

Alex the Statistician

In November 1847, Alex was one of the founding members of the Dublin Statistical Society (later the Statistical and Social Inquiry Society of Ireland). He remained a member for life and was vice president from 1871. He was offered the presidency in 1877 but declined the position supposedly because of pressure of work. In honour of that offer, he instead donated 100 guineas to the Society, to be used solely for the publication of reports on Irish jurisprudence. It is said that there were three reasons for his passing up the role; he shunned publicity; he did not like making speeches, and he was intent on devoting all his energy to the perfection of his beloved directory.

His dedication to the field of statistics is reflected in the development of his immense personal library on all things Irish, a reference source which at the time was said to be more appropriate to the public service than to a private individual. It provided for him information on history, antiquities, statistics, literature, art, science, economics, and social and political conditions of ancient and modern Ireland. Equally, it was said that his directory—the product of his vast library, his understanding of statistics, and his ability to express that data clearly—was unequalled by the efforts of any other individual and was normally the preserve of a national government to issue.

Alex the Family Man

Alex married Maria Dillon (id. 4.001A) in 1824. Maria was the daughter of Columbus Dillon, Esq., of Roscommon, in central Ireland and was always known and referred to as Lady Dillon. Alexander and Maria had nine children, all of whom were baptised at St Mary's Protestant Cathedral, Dublin. Margaret (id. 5.001) was born September and baptised 3 October 1825; Walter (id. 5.002) baptised 27 September 1826; Patrick (id. 5.003) born July and baptised 24 August 1828; Robert (id. 5004) baptised 4 June 1830; Alexander (id. 5.005) born probably in December 1832 and baptised 7 January, 1833; Maria (id. 5.006) born January and baptised 7 February 1834; Walter (id. 5.007) born May 1835 and baptised on the twenty-sixth of that month; Robert (id. 5.008) born 6 May 1837 and baptised nine days later; and finally, Victoria Jane (id. 5.009) born and also baptised in September 1838. That the names Walter and Robert were repeated several years after their first use suggests that the first-named Walter and the first-named Robert both died at a very young age, a common occurrence in those days. Appendix 15 shows the family tree.

In the 1840s, the family home was in Carysfort Avenue, Blackrock, Dublin. In December 1851, a dwelling house at 94

Middle Abbey Street was registered in Alex's name, but whether or not he lived there is not certain. However, it can be said with certainty that the combination of success in the printing business and the size of his growing family enabled and prompted Alex in the 1850s to buy Donnycarney House on the north side of the city, at Fairview.

A portrait of Alex commissioned at the time of the launch of his directory in 1844 and still used in its marketing is shown as Figure 5. Margaret Denton is its custodian. A second portrait, commissioned in 1850 and shown here as Figure 6, is in the care of Hilary Brooks (nee Thom) of Ballygoskin, County Down, Northern Ireland. Both portraits are the work of noted artist Charles Grey (1808-92) of the Royal Hibernian Academy. In 1851, Grey was commissioned by Alex to also paint portraits of his son Patrick and his son-in-law, Frederick Pilkington.

Figure 5: Alex Thom, 1844   Figure 6: Alex Thom, 1850

Alex's wife Maria died in 1867 at Farnham Asylum, Finglas, aged seventy. The death certificate attributed the cause to chronic disease of the brain and noted she had been certified insane for twenty years. Maria was buried in the family vault at Mt Jerome Cemetery, Harold's Cross, Dublin. Her passing and a blossoming relationship between Alex and his then-housekeeper, widow Sarah Mackay, further deteriorated relations between father and sons, Robert in particular, prompting Alex to offer an annuity to him to leave and remain out of Ireland.

Sarah was the third daughter of the late James Ramsey McCulloch, the first professor of political economy at University College, London, from 1828 till 1832. She was also the widow of William Mackay, a Dublin magistrate, with whom she had a son, William Lindsay Mackay. In 1870, Alex returned briefly to his native Scotland to marry Sarah, by now his former housekeeper. She is shown in Figure 7. They married on 16 May of that year at Edinburgh Parish Church. Alex was a little ahead of his time, in that at the time of this second marriage, he arranged a Deed of Settlement (a pre-nuptial agreement) with Sarah. The deed stipulated that in the event of him predeceasing her, she as his unmarried widow would:

(a) retain the use of Donnycarney House, but permit his daughters Maria and Victoria Jane to remain resident there as long as they remained unmarried, and

(b) receive an annuity of £400.

Figure 7: Sarah Thom

Although today there can only be speculation about the compatibility of a couple married 140 years ago, it can reasonably be deduced that Sarah played a significant role in gradually separating Alex from his immediate family. Besides the problem with son Robert alluded to earlier, and Sarah's treatment of Alex's two spinster daughters later in life (see chapter 5), the death of one of Alex's grandchildren in 1874 serves to illustrate the division which had developed within the family. On 5 September 1874, Frederick Pilkington Thom, the six-week-old son of Walter and Mary Anne Thom passed away. Walter and family had moved out of Donnycarney when Alex married Sarah, and were living at 3 Zion Terrace Rathgar in the southern suburbs of Dublin, a containable riding distance from his father's home. But on the day the child died, Alex mailed a rather impersonal letter to his grieving son.

Dear Walter,

Sorry about death of your child. Only two more spaces—for self and wife. Best buy your own plot. My sincere sympathy, in which Mrs Thom joins, believe me, Your affectionate Father.

Alex died five years later at home on Monday, 22 December 1879. Newspapers were generous in their praise of him and his directory, which was considered to be his most significant work. Readers of *The Freeman's Journal* were reminded that:

. . . Alex Thom spared no labour and grudged no expenditure in producing this annual. We have been assured that it never at all recouped the pecuniary outlay; but assuredly, so far as success, appreciation, and universal acknowledgement were a recompense, Mr Thom was abundantly repaid in the only way in which he looked for repayment.

On Friday, 26 December 1879, Alex was buried at Mt. Jerome Cemetery in Dublin, in a gravesite purchased by Sarah and intended for their use alone. In so doing, Sarah had ensured that Alex would be separated from the other members of his family in perpetuity. *The Freeman's Journal* of the following day reported:

The chief mourners were Mr Walter Thom, son of the deceased; Mr W. L. Mackay, stepson; Mr Frederick Pilkington, son-in-law; and Messrs. Frederick C. Pilkington, Hamlet Pilkington, and

Alexander Pilkington, grandsons. The body was enclosed in a coffin of polished oak, mounted with brass.

The funeral was attended by some of the most eminent citizens of Dublin, including the Lord Mayor, the Lord Mayor Elect, the Lord Chancellor and the High Sheriff. The country had lost not only one of its most successful self-made industrialists, but also one of its most knowledgeable and resourceful statisticians. The esteem in which Alex Thom was held by fellow members of his beloved Dublin Statistical Society is reflected in the obituary notice read at its 27 January 1880 meeting and shown as Appendix 9. The last-known photograph of Alex, taken probably in the 1870s, is shown as Figure 8.

Figure 8: Alex Thom in the 1870s

Thom's Directory

Of all of Alex's achievements, the best remembered is his directory. By the early 1840s, Alex was financially secure enough to allow himself to indulge his own personal dream. An Irish directory of his own was his ambition, and having successfully published the *Post Office Directory* for many years, he now spared no expense to achieve his goal.

Thom's *Irish Almanack and Official Directory*, to give its original title, was first published in 1844 with Alex as editor and publisher. The introduction to the first edition began:

In offering a new Almanack and Directory for the notice of the Public, the Publisher is fully sensible that its title to the patronage he hopes for must rest wholly on its intrinsic merits. To the work itself, therefore, he begs leave to refer as the test by which the candid and intelligent tribunal before which it appears will form its decision. When thus examined, its distinctive features will be found to be improved arrangement, novelty of matter, and greater extent of information.

The book contained over 650 pages, 7 1/2 inches by 4 3/4 inches in size, and was hailed by the press as 'the most complete and valuable work of reference and miscellaneous information that has yet appeared in Ireland in the shape of an annual handbook incorporating considerable local statistics on Irish counties and towns'. The famous *Quarterly Review* of the day said: 'It contains more information about Ireland than has been collected in one volume in any country.'

Alex spared neither labour nor expense to improve and enlarge his directory. In 1847, he increased its contents and the size of the pages to 9 inches by 5 1/2 inches, the same page size as today. A list of the nobility, gentry, and traders was added in 1848, and the Annals of Dublin were included the following year. Maria Wootton observes:

One cannot but feel sorry for the proprietors of Pettigrew and Oulton's Directory, its only rival, which was put out of business by 1850. Their publication had made a very creditable effort to provide the public with an extremely useful reference book, which would today be regarded as the father of Thom's Directory. Alex however was in the enviable position of not having to count the cost, and his book's success was immediate. Under his personal supervision it rapidly grew in both prestige and size. The directory never paid for itself in his lifetime; it was subsidized by his very successful printing business.

By 1849, the directory had grown to over 1000 pages, and it had acquired a world-wide reputation as the national handbook of Ireland. In 1852, the *Dublin Street Directory* was included for the first time; today, most Dubliners would not know their home city without it. With each new annual publication, additional data was included, largely due to the efforts of Alex. The modest term of publisher, which Alex adopted in his prefaces, concealed for many years from all but his intimate friends the fact that he was author of the compilation himself, and that the whole conception, plan, and continuous improvements were his. In 1862, he produced a British version titled *Thom's British Directory and Official Handbook for the United Kingdom*, production of which continued until 1873.

Alex disposed of the copyright of his directories business to his son-in-law Frederick Pilkington, in 1877. The main *Dublin Directory* has been revised each year since introduction to this day. The directories have for many decades been a primary reference source for all things Irish for the people of Ireland. A complete set of directories is held in the main reading room of the National Library of Ireland.

It is often said that James Joyce, one of Ireland's more famous authors, had the 1904 edition of the directory at his side as he penned *Ulysses*. Joyce mentions Thom's Directory five times (Refer Penguin Classics 1992 edition.)

Page 156:
Heavy greasy smell there always is in those works. Lukewarm glue in Thom's next door when I was there.

Page 196:
We were in Lombard Street West. Wait, was in Thom's.

Page 445:
A large and appreciative gathering of friends and acquaintances from the metropolis and greater Dublin assembled in their thousands to bid farewell to Nagyasagos uram Lipoti Virag, late of Messrs Alexander Thom's, printers to His Majesty, on the occasion of his departure . . .

Page 492:
Remember about the mistake in the valuation when I was in Thom's.

Page 832:
Catalogue these books. *Thom's Dublin Post Office Directory, 1886.*

In Joyce's obituary in the *Irish Times* in 1941, his friend C. P. Curran stated:

He contained Dublin. If Dublin were destroyed, his could rebuild the houses; if its population were wiped out, his books could repeople it. Joyce was many things, but he was certainly the last forty volumes of Thom's Directory thinking aloud. Alexander Thom would surely have been pleased at this comment.

Thom's Directories is still an active business, publishing an edition covering Dublin and a commercial trade edition covering the nation. The widespread adoption of the Internet has resulted in increasing sales of the data on CDs rather than in book form. Additional information is available on the company's website <thoms.ie>.

Life after Alex

In mid-1879, just months before his death, Alex passed ownership of the company to his son-in-law, Frederick Pilkington. The entry for Alex Thom and Co. in the 1880 edition of *Thom's Almanac*, doubtless drafted before Alex's demise, states that it was 'Printer to the Queen's Most Excellent Majesty, printer and publisher, wholesale stationer and account book manufacturer, agent for the sale of parliamentary papers and Acts of Parliament', indicating Frederick had a thriving business. The development of the firm under Pilkington is covered in *Progress in Irish Printing*, issued by the company itself, in 1936. In summary:

In 1887, it became a Private Limited Company. In 1890, F. C. Pilkington, son of Frederick, floated it into a Public Limited Company. He retired from the Company in 1903, and became Governor of the Bank of Ireland. Then followed a series of amalgamations and take-overs, thus creating a huge company. The 85-90 Middle Abbey Street premises were totally destroyed by fire in the 1916 rebellion, but the business was back in operation very quickly, in temporary accommodation at both 28 Westmoreland Road, and at Crow Street. In 1922 a new factory was opened in Botanic Road, Glasnevin, by which time there were 700 employees, and the factory spread over six acres.

This expansion coincided with the Anglo-Irish Treaty being ratified by the Irish Parliament, provisionally granting autonomy to the Irish Free State. The newly-appointed Post Master General saw it as important that Irish postage stamps should be issued as soon as possible. It was established that a totally-new stamp would take longer than desirable, so it was decided to overprint English stamps with the name of the new Irish Provisional Government. A six weeks' supply of UK stamps arrived on 10 February and, courtesy of prompt work by Alex Thom and Co. Ltd. and another printer assigned the task, were made available to the public one week later, reinforcing the reputation of the company. More details of this exercise are available at <rarebooks.nd.edu/digital/stamps/irish/set1T>.

In 1936, the company moved into carton manufacture and printing. The skeleton of the printing side of the company still exists as Smurfit Thom Spruyt Ltd., of Dublin Industrial Estate, Finglas Road 11, Dublin, manufacturing polythene packaging.

Donnycarney

The name of the home which Alex and his family owned and lived in for fifty years is derived from the Irish 'Domhnach Cearnach' (Carney's Church). Alex purchased Donnycarney in 1853, located five kilometres north of Dublin City's centre. On 29 December 1854, Deed 138 was registered in the Parish of Clontarf, Barony of Coolock, relating to the leasing of land adjacent to Donnycarney. Parties to the deed were the Right Honourable Francis William, Earl of Charlemont, and Alex Thom of Donnycarney. It entitled Thom to rent for farming purposes, eight acres, two roods, and fifteen perches, lately occupied by Henry Davis, for sixty-six years commencing 1 March 1854 at a yearly rental of £50, payable half-yearly each 1 March and 1 September. Another deed, 1855 4 139, entitled Frederick Pilkington for sixty-five years to farm three acres, two roods, and five perches of land at Donnycarney that lately had been in the hands of the same Henry Davis. The yearly rental is not known. Both lots were bounded on the north by the high road leading to Coolock and might well have been adjoining.

Donnycarney remained the family home until it was sold after Sarah died in 1903. The property continued to be used as a private home before the Clontarf Golf Club took possession of the house and land in 1921. The following history of the property was developed by the club:

Donnycarney House was built in 1781 as the residence of Robert Carroll, proprietor of the Donnycarney Quarries. It was from these quarries, located at the 12th, 13th and 14th holes of the current Clontarf Golf Club course, that the black calp stone which was used in the building of Georgian Dublin was quarried.

After six years, Carroll sold it to Daniel Geale, a Marlborough St wholesale merchant and a director of the Royal Exchange Insurance Company. It appears that a certain James Carr carried out stone and brick-laying work on the coach house, stables, hen-house, brick oven and furnace for the sum of £69. 5s. 8d.

In 1819, it became the property of Edward Hamerton, a well-known public notary and stockbroker of the period, who used it as a country residence. On his death in 1832, Donnycarney House was taken over by a man of similar background, Abel Labertouche, who owned a large estate in the West Indies. Bankruptcy, however, forced Labertouche to relinquish the property which was then owned for a short time by a Luke White of County Leitrim before, in 1853, it became the home of Alex Thom, the famous Scottish-born printer who had launched Thom's Almanack and Official Directory in 1844.

Thom, who was Queen Victoria's printer in Ireland, is believed to have employed John Skipton Mulvaney, the celebrated Irish architect of the period, to remodel the house. With his own printing company at 139 Mecklenburgh St. (now Waterford St.) and later at 21 North Earl St., Thom received the lucrative printing contract for the post office for the whole of Ireland in 1833.

Thom died at Donnycarney House on 22 December 1879 and when his widow, Sarah, passed away in 1903, the property came into the possession of Sir Andrew M. Porter, Master of the Rolls, a position to which he was appointed in 1883. Born in Belfast in 1837 and educated at Queen's College, where he received an MA degree, Porter retired to Donnycarney in 1906 and died in 1919.

In August 1921, Reverend John Love Morrow, founder and president of Clontarf Golf Club, received a letter from Porter's widow, Helen. It read:

> Dear Mr Morrow,
>
> As far as one can make plans, we have decided to hold an auction here on September 14th and I propose handing over the keys of Donnycarney House on Saturday the 17th and dismissing the two gardeners, same day. The fields are let for grazing to Mr Hogan till November 1, the end of the lease here. I am telling you this, so that you can make any arrangements you think fit, as unless anything goes wrong, the 17th will see us out.
>
> Yours,
> Helen Porter.

In November 1921, the terms set out by Dublin Corporation for the lease of land attached to Donnycarney House were accepted, and the club had a splendid new home and land for the initial 12-hole course.

Donnycarney House served the club well for seventy years before extensive refurbishment was carried out in 1992. It still offers a homely atmosphere. However, because of the course's location and its appeal to property developers, a proposal in early 2008 was made to the club members to sell the site, to re-establish the club at another location, and to distribute the remaining funds to the members. Newspaper reports suggested that each member would receive a significant cash benefit should they collectively approve the proposal. The global financial uncertainty which surfaced later that year, together with club member sentiment, resulted in the proposal being shelved. Since then, the club has embarked on a major refurbishment of its clubhouse, endeavouring to recreate the façade and the colours of Donnycarney of the 1850s. Barbara Barrett (nee Thom) of New Ross, Eire, is custodian of a landscape water colour painting of Donnycarney House as it existed then, and shown as Figure 9. The artist was Charles Grey. Prints are held by each of Barbara's sisters, and another is mounted in the lobby of the clubhouse. Notes on the back of the original state the figures in the foreground (l to r) represent Alex's daughter Maria; John Bolton, the future father-in-law of Alex's son Walter; the artist, and a Mrs Price and daughter, possibly members of the family of Alex's bookkeeper.

Figure 9: Donnycarney House

Clontarf Golf Club celebrated its centenary on 21 July 2012, at the clubhouse; celebration of the centenary of its occupation of Donnycarney itself will have to wait for another nine years.

CHAPTER 4

THE LEGACIES

Alex's Will

On 19 June 1877, Alex Thom made his last will and testament, in which he:

(a) Appointed his wife Sarah, his son-in-law Frederick Pilkington, W. N. Hancock, G. Atkinson, and his stepson William Lindsay Mackay as executors and trustees of his will;

(b) Revoked the Deed of Settlement made at the time of his marriage to Sarah, which had entitled his daughters Maria and Victoria Jane to reside at Donnycarney House whilst they remained unmarried;

(c) Denied the right of his daughters to reside at Donnycarney House;

(d) Bequeathed Donnycarney House, plus the grounds, horses, carriages, cattle, furniture, books, plate, jewellery, linen, china, pictures, and goods and chattels to Sarah, absolutely;

(e) In the event of Sarah pre-deceasing him, bequeathed Donnycarney House etc. as above to his stepson William Lindsay Mackay;

(f) Bequeathed all his stocks and shares to Sarah, or should she predecease him, to his stepson;

(g) Bequeathed an annuity of £500 for life to his son Walter and after his death to his wife Mary Ann, for so long as she remains his widow;

(h) Bequeathed an annuity of £200 to his son Robert for life or for so long as he shall remain out of Ireland, and after his death, £100 to his wife for as long as she remains his widow and remains out of Ireland;

(i) Bequeathed an annuity of £200 for life to his daughter Maria, and an annuity of £150 for life to his daughter Victoria Jane;

(j) Bequeathed his gold repeater watch to his grandson Alexander, son of his son Walter;

(k) Bequeathed 100 Guineas to each executor of his will;

(l) Bequeathed the goodwill of the printing and publishing business, and the buildings, plant, and equipment to his daughter Margaret (2/3 share) and to his grandson Frederick Coddington Pilkington (1/3 share);

(m) Granted Margaret and Frederick Coddington Pilkington the opportunity to buy the business's stock of books and paper at favourable specified rates;

(n) Directed the trustees to continue to pay the premiums on two life insurance policies totalling £2500 favouring his son Walter;

(o) Directed that all the remaining estate, after payment of administration and funeral, etc. expenses and all legacies and annuities as defined be paid to his son Walter; and

(p) Directed that in the event of his daughters Maria and Victoria Jane being asked to vacate Donnycarney House, and not vacating within one month, their annuities be revoked.

Nine months later, on 3 March 1878, Alex made a codicil to his will, specifying that:

(a) The goodwill of the printing and publishing business, and the buildings, plant and equipment be shared with two-fifths to Margaret, one-fifth to Frederick Coddington Pilkington, and two-fifths to his friend Edward Thomas Lefroy of Ossory Lodge, Sandymount, Co Dublin;

(b) The said Edward Thomas Lefroy be appointed a trustee and executor of the will and that he be given £100, the same as the initial trustees, and

(c) All other conditions of the original will would still apply.

Eighteen months later, on 17 September 1879, Alex made a second codicil to his will. Since writing the first codicil, both his daughter Margaret and Edward Thomas Lefroy had died. Alex specified that:

(a) The goodwill of the printing and publishing business and the buildings plant and equipment be passed to his grandson Frederick Coddington Pilkington, in exchange for £20,000, to be paid within six months of Alex's death. In the event of this payment not being made, the trustees were to sell the business;

(b) Of the £20000 payment, or the proceeds of sale, £8000 was to be set aside for annuities, legacies, and life insurance premium payments, with any excess to go to his son Walter;

(c) The remaining £12000 or so be bequeathed to his wife, Sarah, or in the event of her predeceasing him, to his stepson, William Lindsay Mackay;

(d) £1000 be bequeathed to his eldest grandson, Alexander Pilkington, son of Frederick Pilkington;

(e) £500 be bequeathed to his bookkeeper, James Henry Price;

(f) The appointment of his son-in-law, Frederick Pilkington, as trustee or executor be revoked, 'feeling it might place him in an invidious position', and

(g) All other conditions of the original will and first codicil would still apply.

A mere ten weeks later, on 4 December 1879, Alex made a third codicil to his will. It recognised that he had in fact sold the printing and publishing business in its entirety to his son-in-law Frederick Pilkington, for £18000 plus an annuity of £1500 for the rest of his life. Of the £18000, a partial payment of £12000 was paid and invested in securities. The remaining £6000 was due on 15 February 1880. Accordingly, the codicil recorded this arrangement and specified that:

(a) All prior bequests in respect of the printing and publishing business be revoked;

(b) The outstanding £6000 be considered to be part of his remaining estate; and

(c) All funds in his current accounts be bequeathed to his wife, Sarah, so that she would not want for funds in the short term after his death.

Alexander died just eighteen days later on 22 December 1879. On 27 January 1880, his will (with codicils) was declared for probate. The total estate was valued at £100,000, on which £1350 probate duty was paid.

Sarah's Will

On 28 May 1903, Sarah Thom made her last will and testament, in which she:

(a) Directed that she be buried in Mt. Jerome Cemetery in ground already purchased by her;

(b) Bequeathed £50 life annuities to her maid, Maggie Meade, and to her coachman, Patrick Neill;

(c) Bequeathed £100 to each of Patrick Neill's sons, William Neill and Patrick Neill. If under age, the funds were to be entrusted to the parents for the children's advancement;

(d) Bequeathed £500 to her former servant, Mary Leighton;

(e) Bequeathed £20 to her former servant, Eliza McGrath;

(f) Bequeathed £50 to her outdoor servant, James Clark;

(g) Bequeathed to all servants in her employ at time of death, six months wages; these to include Patrick Neill, groom Patrick Kearon, gardener Joseph Martin, and James Clark;

(h) Directed that the residence Donnycarney House and adjoining grounds, household furniture linen and books not specifically disposed of by her will, her carriage horses, farming stock, and outdoor effects, including stable furniture, harnesses, etc. be sold by her executors;

(i)   Directed that her plate, plated ware, jewellery, china ornaments, and articles of virtue not specifically disposed of by her will, be sold in London at Christie and Manson's or some other auctioneers of standing;

(j)   Directed that the Japanese Collection or such articles of same not given away by her be presented by her executors to the Science and Art Museum, Kildare Street, Dublin, to be placed together in said museum and called the Thom Collection;

(k)   Directed that all the books which belonged to Alex be presented to the National Library of Ireland and called the Alexander Thom Collection;

(l)   Bequeathed the four paintings in her dining room to her friend Thomas Henry Longfield;

(m) Bequeathed the following charitable legacies £1000 each:

Royal Victoria Eye and Ear Hospital
Stewart Institution for Idiotic and Imbecile Children
Hospital for Incurables, Donnybrook
Adelaide Hospital, Peters Street, Dublin
National Hospital for Consumption, near Newcastle, Co Wicklow
Richmond Whitworth and Hardwicke Combined Hospital, Dublin;

(n)   Bequeathed to Sir Patrick Dun's Hospital, Dublin, £500;

(o)   Bequeathed to the National Children's Hospital, Dublin, £250;

(p)   Bequeathed to the Orthopaedic Hospital, Brunswick St., Dublin, £250;

(q)   Directed that a bed be provided and maintained in the following hospitals and called 'The Mackay Bed' in memory of her son the late William Mackay:

Royal Victoria Eye and Ear Hospital
National Hospital for Consumption
Richmond Whitworth and Hardwicke Combined Hospital;

(r)   Directed that a bed be provided and maintained in each of the other hospitals except the National Children's Hospital and the Orthopaedic Hospital, and called 'The Thom Bed';

(s)   Directed that all taxes and duties on the above legacies be paid by the executors of the will;

(t)   Bequeathed to the children of the late Robert Thom of Geelong and their children living at the time of her death, £5000, divided equally;

(u)   Bequeathed to the children of Walter Thom of Cullen House, Slane, and their children living at the time of her death, £10000, divided equally;

(v)   Bequeathed to the children of her late sister Isabella Black, and to Ella McLennan, daughter of her late sister Mary McLennan, £5000 each;

(w)   Bequeathed to her friend Mrs Annie Caton, formerly Ivory, £1000;

(x)   Bequeath to Walter Scott Junior, godson of her son, £1000;

(y)   Bequeathed to Ernest Scott and to each of the other sons of Walter Scott and of the late Isabella Scott, formerly Cox, of Liverpool, £500 each;

(z)   Bequeathed to her friend Mary Elizabeth Longfield as a token of esteem and regard, £2000;

(aa) Bequeathed to Arthur Cox of Birmingham, £300;

(bb) Bequeathed to Miss A Joy, £300;

(cc) Bequeathed to James Little MD, £1000;

(dd) Bequeathed to Sir William Thomson CB, £1000;

(ee) Bequeathed to Miss Annie E O'Grady, late of 48 Upper Sackville St. Dublin, £500;

(ff) Bequeathed to each of her executors, £1000;

(gg) Directed that all remaining estate be divided equally between:

Royal Victoria Eye and Ear Hospital
Stewart Institution for Idiotic and Imbecile Children
Adelaide Hospital
National Hospital for Consumption
Richmond Whitworth and Hardwicke Combined Hospital:

(hh) Appointed as executors of her will:

Walter Scott of Sefton Park, Liverpool
Lucius Hutton of Fitzwilliam Place, Dublin
Professor Daniel Cunningham of Edinburgh University
Thomas Henry Longfield, FSA, and
Robert Ormsby Longfield of Harcourt St., Dublin;

(ii) Directed that the firm of solicitors associated with Mr R. O. Longfield be engaged to handle legal issues associated with her property.

Later the same day, she issued a codicil to the will, in which she:

(a) Bequeathed to Walter Thom, the painting of her late husband Alex;

(b) Bequeathed to her very dear and valued friend, Robert Ormsby Longfield, £6000 free of legacy duty, plus the picture of her father which was in her bedroom and the secretaire and bookcase and books in her late son's sitting room, such bequests being additional to those in her will;

(c) Bequeathed to her dear friend, Cecelia Black, the walnut chest of drawers in her bedroom with the books on it;

(d) Bequeathed to her executors as joint tenants, the grave which she had purchased in Mt. Jerome Cemetery.

Three months later, on 4 September 1903, she issued a second codicil to her will. In it, she revoked the bequest of a £50 annuity to Patrick Neill and the bequests of £100 each to Patrick Neill's children William Neill and Patrick Neill.

Sarah died two weeks later on 20 September 1903, having survived Alex by twenty-three years. In line with her will, she was buried in Mt. Jerome Cemetery, alongside him and the son from her first marriage, William Mackay, who had died of pneumonia a few months earlier.

It is not altogether surprising that of Sarah's considerable estate, the only bequests to her step-children's families were £5000 to the family of the late Robert in Australia, and £10000 and a portrait of Alexander to the family of Walter of Cullen. Her surviving stepdaughter Victoria Jane received nothing; nor did the surviving progeny of her late stepdaughter Margaret (Pilkington), whom she might have considered were already independently wealthy.

In accordance with Clause (i) of Sarah's will, her jewellery was auctioned in London. An unidentifiable newspaper in an article headed 'Sale of a Dublin Lady's Jewels' reported thus:

London, Thursday.

Messrs Christie, Manson, and Woods sold at their salerooms, King Street, St James's, today the magnificent casket of jewels, the property of the late Mrs Sarah Thom, of Donnycarney House, Co. Dublin. The following were the prices of the principal lots:-

A collet necklace, composed of 43 large graduated brilliants and single brilliant snap, £1500.

A brilliant circular cluster pendant with a large round brilliant in the centre, surrounded by eight smaller stones and double collet snap, also forming bracelet, with gold mount or hair ornament, £1,200.

A brilliant pendant Latin cross composed of eleven large stones and trefoil brilliant loop, £570.

A sapphire and brilliant cluster and scroll tiara, with small brilliant bandeau to form necklace, and mounts to form three cluster brooches or hair ornaments, £780.

A five row pearl necklace composed of small, round, graduated pearls, with seed pearls strung between, and pearl and brilliant cluster snap, and with brilliant bars with three oval opal and brilliant cluster pendants also forming brooches, £335.

The Thom Collection—National Museum of Ireland

In accordance with Clause (j) of Sarah's will, the entire bequest of 496 Japanese items is included in open display at the National

Museum's Decorative Arts and History Department at Collins Barracks, Dublin. However the items currently are not tagged and are included with items from other bequests, making specific identification difficult. The Art and Industrial Department's handwritten inventory is headed 'Thom Collection', and an extract from the twenty-seven-page inventory is shown as Appendix 10. Its preamble states:

The following objects numbered 371 to 867-05 form the Thom Collection of Japanese objects and were bequeathed to the museum by Mrs Thom per T. H. Longfield, F. S. A. (Keeper, Art and Industrial Collections), according to whose advice principally the collection was formed.

The collection was deemed sufficiently important that on 5 March 1985, at the re-opening of the Japanese Room after forty years out of service, the visiting Crown Prince Akihito and Crown Princess Michiko of Japan viewed the collection. The display was part of an exhibition 'Decorative Arts of Japan'. The *Irish Times* newspaper reported the following day that only 200 specimens of the 1500 pieces in total were displayed. 'Most of it was acquired around the turn of the century—the Duke of Leinster and Mrs Thom being the major donors.'

The Thom Bequest—National Library of Ireland

In accordance with Clause (k) of Sarah's will, the entire Alex Thom private library of 3900 volumes is held in the National Library at Kildare St., Dublin. It is retained in secure storage, but restricted access to it is permitted. The entire inventory is recorded in a sixty-four-page listing headed 'Thom Bequest. Schedule of Books transferred at Christmas 1903 in accordance with the will of Mrs Alexander Thom'. Appendix 11 shows the front page of the inventory. Additional information is available at <nli. ie.collections>.

CHAPTER 5

THE FAMILY SPREADS ITS WINGS

The lives of the nine children of Alex and Maria varied significantly. Four of them continued the bloodline, with three of them carrying the family name into the sixth generation. Three migrated from Ireland, each to a separate country.

Margaret Thom (id. 5.001)

Margaret married into the Pilkington family, whose Irish roots had been established generations earlier. She died in 1878, a year before her father died. The history of the Pilkington branch is related in chapter 6.

Walter Thom (id. 5.002)

Walter was christened 27 September 1826. Given that another child was given the same name nine years later, as was common in those days of high infant mortality, it is highly likely that this Walter died in infancy. No burial records have been located, but he almost certainly would have been buried in Dublin.

Patrick Thom (id. 5.003)

Until recently, Patrick was the mystery man; nothing was known about him other than that he was born in 1828, and his portrait resides with Rosemary Coffey (nee Thom) in Killinchy, County Down, Northern Ireland. Research of artist Charles Grey who had painted at least two portraits of Patrick's father Alex, confirmed he was responsible also for the 1851 portrait of Patrick, shown as Figure 10.

Figure 10: Patrick Thom

Patrick's business career has many open issues. In all likelihood, he worked initially with his father in the family business. The Dublin Registry of Deeds shows that in 1853, he established a company partnership (Index 7/296). The following year, the type-founding company Marr, Thom and Co. rented property at 87 Middle Abbey St. from Alexander Thom (Index 28/221), and in 1855, Patrick and Marr had another deed (Index 32/55), possibly after the collapse of their partnership. That Patrick did not continue a career with his father is perhaps a reflection of the problems often associated with family relationships in a business environment.

Patrick married Sidney Thornburgh Browne (id. 5.003A) of Drumcondra, daughter of Henry Thornburgh Browne, solicitor, at the Church of St Mary, Dublin, in 1854. The 1858 edition of the Post Office Dublin Directory listed 25 Leinster Square, Rathmines as his residence. The 1860 edition of his father's *Thom's Directory* had Patrick living at 3 Berkeley Street Lower. On 21 May 1863, he and his wife were sponsors at the christening in the Church of St Mary, Dublin, of a Nicholaus Franciscus Patritius McVeigh. Both the 1867 and 1869 directory editions showed him living at 3 Rathmines Park before he departed Ireland permanently.

Exactly when and why Patrick moved to the Isle of Man remains a mystery. The island is located in the Irish Sea, a mere twenty miles off the southern coast of Scotland, thirty miles east of Northern Ireland, and eighty miles north-east of Dublin, and has an area of 221 square miles. Current population is only 80,000, predominantly of British stock, so the island would have been sparsely populated 150 years ago. It was then, and remains today, a self-governing British Crown Dependency, with its own government and its own currency. The capital is the city of Douglas.

One-year-old daughter Sidney Frances Thornburgh Thom (id. 6.015) died in December 1870 and was buried on the island in the parish of Braddan. Patrick died less than two months later, and also was buried at Braddan. The family tree is included in Appendix 15.

To date, nothing is known of the fate of his wife or other children, if any. It seems odd that an only child would be born fifteen years into the marriage. However, that Patrick's portrait finished up in the hands of his brother Walter and still resides within that branch of the family suggests Patrick himself outlived his wife and all offspring.

Robert Thom (id. 5.004)

Robert was christened 4 June 1830. As with Walter above, he almost certainly died in infancy, as the name was given to another sibling born in 1837. Robert's burial site is not known, but most likely is in Dublin.

Alexander Thom (id. 5.005)

Other than for his christening at the Church of St Mary, Dublin, on 7 January 1833, nothing is known of Alexander. He is not buried at Mt. Jerome, which opened in 1836 and became the preferred family cemetery. Portraits of a number of his siblings were commissioned in the 1850s, but none is known to exist for Alexander. He was not a beneficiary of his father's will written in 1877. Research continues.

Maria Thom (id. 5.006)

Maria neither married nor had children. Alex's 1877 will granted Maria a lifetime annuity of £200, together with residency rights to Donnycarney House for as long as she remained single. Codicils later removed that right to residency, probably under pressure from second wife Sarah, and the annuity continued only if Maria vacated the family home within one month of being served such notice. With the passing of her husband, Sarah exercised that right swiftly; Maria was living at 132 Queens Road, Bayswater, London, by early 1880. She died in 1903, aged sixty-nine, at 48 Waterloo Road, Dublin, most likely her residence at the time. She died six months before Sarah but was not going to be a beneficiary of her will anyway. Barbara Barrett is custodian of a portrait of Maria, circa 1860, shown as Figure 11.

Figure 11: Maria Thom

Walter Thom (id. 5.007)

Walter's bloodline is carried by descendants in England, Ireland and Northern Ireland, where the Thom name ultimately was lost (see chapter 7), and in Argentina, where the family name continues into the ninth generation (see chapter 8).

Robert Thom (id. 5.008)

Robert's bloodline is carried by descendants in Australia, where the Thom name continues into the ninth generation (see chapter 9).

Victoria Jane Thom (id. 5.009)

Victoria Jane neither married nor had children. Her annuity from Alex was £150. Her residency rights to Donnycarney House were the same as those of her sister Maria. After her father's death, she too was forced from the family home and lived at Newberry Hall, County Kildare, courtesy of her brother-in-law Frederick Pilkington, who by then was a widower. Where she lived after Frederick died in 1898 is not known. She survived her stepmother Sarah by eleven years, but was not a beneficiary of her will. She died in 1914, aged seventy-five years, and was buried at Mt. Jerome, Dublin. Hilary Brooks is custodian of a portrait of Victoria Jane, circa 1860, shown as Figure 12.

Figure 12: Victoria Jane Thom

Mount Jerome Cemetery, Dublin

This cemetery holds more members of the Thom family than any other in the world. It is located in the suburb of Harold's Cross, on the south side of the city, just beyond the Grand Canal. It was the first privately-owned cemetery in Ireland when it opened in 1836. Since then, it has accepted 250,000 burials, making it the second largest burial site in the country. Cremations commenced a decade ago, and 10,000 have been conducted to date. Mt. Jerome Cemetery accepted only Protestants until the 1920s, when Roman Catholic burials became accepted. At least fifteen members of the greater Thom family are buried at Mt. Jerome.

The first family burial there was that of Maria, the first wife of Alexander the printer. Alex purchased perpetual burial rights for the 8ft 6in x 6ft Plot 3504 in Section C92 for £12.10s.0d. He paid £45.2s.6d for an underground vault with capacity for six, no doubt thinking ahead for not only his own ultimate fate, but also that of at least some of his family. Maria's burial service conducted 21 March 1867 cost £1.1s.0d.

The vault is now full but does not include the remains of Alex; second wife Sarah saw to that. Others interred therein are:

Sarah Thom, 1873. She was a daughter of Alex's son Walter and Mary Anne Ruxton, and died aged two.

Walter Thom, 1886. He was the second son of Walter and Mary Anne Ruxton, and died aged twenty.

Walter Thom 1909. He was the seventh child of Alex the printer, and died aged seventy-four.

Victoria Jane Thom 1914. She was the youngest daughter of Alex the printer, and died aged seventy-five.

Mary Anne Ruxton Thom, 1921. She died aged eighty-three.

Time has eroded any markings on the vault, making it difficult to locate. Proceed from the chapel along Hawthorn Walk and then turn right into the Long Walk. The vault is on the right hand side, located two plots beyond the Salmon grave, and five plots before the Peter Jackson above-ground vault.

When Alex the printer, died in 1879, his widow Sarah paid £70 for the perpetual rights to burial in Plot 5372 in Section C115. She then arranged a much grander grave for him than the family vault, with the intention of her sharing it with him upon her demise, as specified in her will. But she had not anticipated that her son, William Lindsay Mackay, would predecease her. He died a few months earlier than she, aged fifty-two, and is buried there also. The reddish-brown Aberdeen granite headstone, with clear inscriptions, enables the ten-foot square grave to be readily identified. It is located ten metres off to the right of the Long Walk, and approximately another twenty-five metres beyond the Thom family vault. The other six Thom family members at Mt. Jerome are at three double gravesites:

Section C3, Plot 4512

Frederick Pilkington Thom, 1874. He was a son of Walter and Mary Anne Ruxton Thom, and died aged less than two months. A receipt exists in the family files for £7.0s.0d total cost of burial. Hubert Ernest Thom, 1875. He was another son of Walter and Mary Anne Ruxton Thom, and died aged three weeks.

Section B+3, Plot 162-11624

Maria Thom, 1903. She was the second daughter of Alex the printer, and died aged sixty-nine.

Maria Victoria Elizabeth Thom, 1910. She was the only daughter of Walter and Mary Anne Ruxton Thom who survived till adulthood. She died aged forty.

Section C39, Plot 17291

Henry Bentley Thom, 1926. He was the eldest son of Dillon Turner and Mary Evelyn Thom, and died aged twenty-six.

Mary Evelyn Thom, 1934. She was the first wife of Dillon Turner Thom, and died aged sixty-seven.

The more recent burials of Dublin-based Thom family members have been at Deansgrange Cemetery.

CHAPTER 6

THE PILKINGTONS

This chapter relates to Margaret (id. 5.001), the firstborn of Alex and Maria and the only daughter to have continued the family line, if not the name. The Pilkington branch of the family tree has been the most difficult to research and is incomplete, but with ongoing investigation.

When I first met Bolton Thom in 1977, he mentioned that his branch and the Pilkington branch had not communicated since the late 1800s, even though both branches lived in Ireland. The stated reason was the unequal distribution of family wealth as dictated in the will of Alexander Thom the printer, which arguably favoured the Pilkingtons, into whose family his daughter Margaret had married. Bolton and his brother Alex, both of whom were born in the early 1900s, grew up not knowing their second cousins. In the early stages of my research into the wider family, and particularly the Pilkington branch, Bolton could tell me only what he had gleaned from newspapers saved over the years by his father and which essentially was limited to news concerning the immediate descendants of Margaret and Frederick Pilkington. Bolton understood there to be three sons, all of whom attended their grandfather's funeral.

Genealogical research is much easier starting with the current generation and working backwards in time, than starting with an early generation and working forward to the current generation, the situation I faced with the Pilkington branch. This is because birth and death certificates generally specify parental data but not necessarily the data of progeny. Interestingly, I can remember from that 1977 visit to Ireland, Alex relating how one day whilst in a barber's chair, he heard another customer telling somebody he was a Pilkington descendant of Alex Thom the printer. For whatever reason, Alex either was not able, or did not attempt, to introduce himself to his distant relative. If only . . .

Now let's fast forward to 2010 and the Internet age. Research revealed Newberry Hall, the former Pilkington family home, had been sold just a few months earlier by Richard Robinson, whose grandfather Richard had purchased it from the Pilkingtons in 1911. Indirect communication with Richard resulted in him lending me a copy of *Harland's History and Pedigrees of the Pilkingtons* by R. G. Pilkington, coincidentally published in 1906 by Alex Thom and Co. (Limited) of Dublin. Its title page is shown as Appendix 12. The book traces the global history of the Pilkington family, commencing in the days of the Norman Conquest. Coverage of the relevant Irish branches of the family commences page 128 as below:

The Pilkingtons of Newberry Hall and The Haggard County Kildare, Westbury County Dublin, and Rathbody County Louth

The records of this family commence with the town land of Rathbody, near Tallinstown in County Louth. Rev. Miles Pilkington of Branganstown in County Louth, in 1726, gave a lease of twenty-five years renewable to Brent Pilkington of Rathbody, Louth, Gent, containing fifteen acres. Edward Pilkington of Grange, County Louth, in 1745, deals with Great Rathbody, County Louth, and in 1749, Edward Pilkington of Rathbody deals with seventy-five acres of Arthurstown and fifty-five acres of Rathbody. In a deed in 1779, Henry Pilkington, then of Rathbody, Gentleman, and Brent Pilkington, late of Rathbody are mentioned.

Joseph Pilkington of Louth, described as son of Edward Pilkington, entered Trinity College at the age of seventeen on 2 November 1769 and became a clergyman; and his son Joseph, of Louth, entered College in 1799, aged eighteen. The latter also became a clergyman, and as chaplain to the British Embassy on his way to Madrid, on board the *Bellerophon* man-of-war, he was present when the great Napoleon surrendered to the English in 1815. He subsequently became rector of Langfield, in the County of Tyrone, and by his wife, Fanny, daughter of Rev. William Coddington, rector of Kilmore, County Meath, had six sons, one of whom, the late Frederick Pilkington, J.P., D.L.(Deputy Lieutenant), of Newberry Hall, County Kildare, married Margaret, daughter of Alexander Thom, Esq., of Donnycarney Hall, County Dublin. Three of his sons, Alexander, father of Lionel Pilkington, now of Newberry Hall; Frederick Coddington Pilkington, J.P., D.L., now of Westbury, County Dublin (who lost his only son in the Boer

War on 6 October 1901); and Edward, son of Sir William Hancock Pilkington, J.P., of 'The Haggard', Carbury, County of Kildare, now represent this branch of the Pilkingtons. The daughters have married into the well-known and well-connected families of Mayne, Ormsby, Hornidge, Scrope, Rynd, Lyons, and Gregg.

Included in Pilkington's book are family tree charts, the data of which in some instances conflicts with both the text and reality; Additional information from various external sources has enabled those conflicts to be resolved, e.g. Edward was the brother and not the son of William Handcock, resulting in the Pilkington family tree shown as Appendix 16. The story of the Pilkington/Thom marriage and family, which in Pilkington history terms commences as Generation 23 and in Thom history terms as Generation 5, is related below.

Very little is known of Margaret's childhood and young adult life. As the eldest of nine children born over a thirteen-year period, she doubtless would have played a significant role in the development of her younger siblings. At the time of her marriage in 1844, the family home was in Carysfort Avenue, Blackrock, Dublin. Her marriage to Frederick Pilkington was celebrated in the Church of St. Thomas, Dublin. A witness to the solemnisation was William Ball, whose family name may have been the inspiration for the second given name of their second daughter. In addition to Frederick's family history outlined above, it should be noted that his paternal grandmother was a Wade, which name continues to appear as a given name in later generations, as does the Coddington maiden family name of his mother.

Margaret and Frederick had not three children as understood by Bolton Thom, but eleven, over a twenty-year period. All survived to adulthood: Margaret Elizabeth (id. 6.001) was born in 1845;

Alexander (id. 6.002) in June 1846; Frances Ball (id. 6.003) in circa 1848; Frederick Coddington (id. 6.004) in 1849; Maria (id. 6.005) in circa 1851; Olivia Wade (id. 6.006) in circa 1853; Hamlet Wade (id. 6.007) in 1854; William Handcock (id. 6.008) in 1859; Edward Shenton (id. 6.009) in circa 1861; Eveline Maud (id. 6.010) in circa 1862; and Violet Josephine (id. 6.011) in 1864. In 1850, the family had registered addresses at 89 Middle Abbey St., Dublin, and 3 Prince's St. North. In 1854, the family lived at Maryville, Castleknock, Dublin. Four years later, they moved to St John's, Donnycarney. In about 1870, Margaret and Frederick purchased Newberry Hall, Carbury, County Kildare, and made it their permanent family home. Margaret died there in 1878 and is buried in the grounds of the local Church of Ireland church.

Frederick had a good work ethic and a flair for business. Operating from his Prince's Street premises immediately behind Middle Abbey Street where his father-in-law Alex operated, Frederick provided bookbinding services to the Queen and the Lord Lieutenant, the university, and the Royal Irish Academy. In 1848, he took out a lease of 89 Middle Abbey Street, going right through to Prince's Street, at a yearly rental of £73.16s.11d. paid to John Mowat. In complete contrast to the attitude of his brothers-in-law Walter and Robert, Frederick had enthusiastically embraced a genuine interest in the operation of Alex's printing business. This interest was rewarded handsomely by Alex later in life, as is evident in the final codicil to his will. Alex sold the entire printing and publishing business to his son-in-law for £18,000 plus an annuity of £1500, and then died later that month.

In addition to active involvement in the family business, Frederick committed considerable time to duties for the public good. He served as a Justice of the Peace in Dublin, and reached the rank of Deputy Lieutenant of County Kildare. Over time, Frederick passed control of the business to his eldest surviving son, Frederick Coddington Pilkington, and died in the family home in 1898, twenty years after his wife. He is buried alongside her at Carbury. His will is summarised in Appendix 13. The estate was valued for probate at £64861.14s.4d., on which was paid estate duty and interest of £4477.7s.2d.

Margaret Elizabeth Pilkington (id. 6.001)

Margaret Elizabeth, the first child of Margaret and Frederick, was born in Dublin. In 1865, she married Dr Robert St John Mayne, of 29 Grenville St., Dublin, the son of surgeon Dr Robert Mayne. They had three daughters: Aida Constance (id. 7.001), born in 1868, Florence Ethel (id. 7.002), born in 1869, and May Josephine Sedborough (id. 7.003), whose birth date is not known. Sedborough was the name of the Mayne ancestral home, near Mt. Sedborough, County Fermanagh, Northern Ireland, and where an ancestor, John Mayne, had been murdered in front of his wife by Irish rebels in 1641. Margaret Elizabeth's husband died in 1874, aged thirty-one. She remarried the following year; her second husband was John Arthur Cooper Ormsby, Esq. of Burlington House, Burlington Road, Dublin, son of William Ormsby, Esq. Ormsby had been Sub-Sheriff for Sligo and inspector of local prisons before moving to Dublin. Prior to this marriage, Margaret Elizabeth and family had been living with her sisters Frances and Olivia at 8 Rutland Square East, Dublin. The marriage was solemnised at the Church of St George, Dublin, and produced another two girls, Arabella Mabel Nicholson (id. 7.006), born in 1876, and Margaret Muriel (id. 7.011), born in 1880. Nicholson was a family name, which Arabella normally did not use.

The Irish Census conducted 31 March 1901 recorded both parents, the two youngest girls, and Aida Mayne (correctly listed as Ormsby's step-daughter) residing that night at 5 Artaine West, Drumcondra Rural, Dublin. Ormsby described himself as Senior Sheriff of Dublin. The next Irish Census on 2 April 1911 listed Ormsby as an Under-Sheriff as well as a civil engineer, and the family's residential address as 23 Raglan Road, Pembroke West.

Certainly, the four eldest daughters married. In 1905 at the Drumcondra Church of Ireland, Aida, then living locally at Elm Park, married Arthur Forde Pilson, a major in the Royal Dublin Fusiliers, and living in the Barracks, Naas, Kildare. The 1911 Census showed them living at 47 Bridge St., Downpatrick, County Down, without family. Given that Aida was forty-two by then (though modestly recorded in the census as only thirty-five versus Arthur's correctly recorded forty-five years), it is likely that they died without issue. No progeny has been traced.

Florence and May had joint weddings at Carbury Church of Ireland on 14 October 1892. Florence, then residing at Newberry Hall, married Smith Ramadge Ramadge, gentleman of The Woodhouse, Rostrevor, County Down, the son of Smith Ramadge, a captain in the Irish Buffs (Twenty-eighth Regiment). She became a widow within a few years and then remarried in 1899 at Drumcondra, Dublin. Her second husband, John Hall, gentleman of The Needles, Howth, was the son of another John Hall, barrister. Neither Florence nor her husband appeared in either the 1901 or 1911 Irish Censuses.

May, also of Newberry Hall, married William Henry Edward Woodwright, from Ballybay, County Monaghan, who together with his elder brother Charles Sharman Woodwright had been a student boarder at Windermere College, Applethwaite, Westmoreland, England, at the time of the 1881 Census. Woodwright was the son of Charles Patrick Woodwright, a colonel in the Irish Army. He qualified as a Licentiate of the Royal College of Surgeons (Ireland) in 1886. He was appointed a surgeon in the Indian Medical Service in October 1887 and was immediately assigned to the Hazara Expedition of 1888, a military campaign by the British against the tribes of Kala Dhaka in the Hazara region of what is now Pakistan. He then was appointed Medical Officer in Charge of the First Punjab Cavalry. In May 1892, he became a Fellow of the Royal College of Surgeons of Ireland. He and May married in the joint wedding ceremony mentioned earlier, before returning to India. After several regimental postings, he was appointed major in 1899. Thereafter, he held various positions as a civil, jail, and lunatic asylum surgeon, achieving the rank of lieutenant-colonel in October 1907. He retired on 10 July 1920, his fifty-fifth birthday. In 1928, he dedicated a plaque to his wife's memory at Carbury Church, as described later in this chapter. A clasp awarded to him for participating in the Hazara Expedition was auctioned by Spink in London in 2000.

Arabella Mabel, of Elm Park Drumcondra, married Ralph Smith Oliver Cusack in the local parish church in 1905. Cusack, a civil engineer, was the son of James William Cusack, gentleman, and lived at Frelyon, Ilford, Essex. The marriage ended and Cusack remarried, dying in 1965 without issue from either marriage. He had achieved the rank of major within the Royal Army Service Corps. Research continues on Arabella.

The fate of the youngest daughter, Margaret Muriel, is not known. She is recorded in both the 1901 and 1911 Irish Censuses as being single and living with her parents.

In 1925, the Northern Ireland Land Act was approved, which enabled the acquisition of privately-owned land by the Land Purchase Commission. The 11 April 1930 edition of the *Belfast Gazette* listed fourteen properties of total area 660 acres, all within the County of Fermanagh, and owned (presumably jointly) by May Woodwright, Aida Pilson, and John Hall. Fermanagh was the home county of the Mayne family, so it is reasonable to conclude that those properties were bequeathed to the three daughters of Robert St John Mayne by their mother Margaret Elizabeth, who died in 1923, the year after her second husband died. By the time of the enforced land acquisition, May Woodwright had died. In all likelihood, Florence Ethel had died too, leaving her second husband, John Hall, as the beneficiary.

Frederick Pilkington in his will written in 1897 made specific bequests direct to the three daughters of Margaret Elizabeth's first marriage, but his charity did not extend to the children from the second marriage—Arabella and Margaret. Nonetheless, they doubtless would have been beneficiaries of their mother's will.

An interesting coincidence which surfaced during this research is that a John Hall and family were recorded in the 1901 Census as residing at Carbury Demesne (Newberry Hall). He was employed as a coachman and domestic servant, and his wife Sarah, as housekeeper.

Alexander Pilkington (id. 6.002)

Alexander, the first son of Margaret and Frederick, and the first grandson of Alex the printer, was born in Carbury in 1846.

He was one of only two grandsons benefiting from Alex's will and was bequeathed £1000.

In 1875 in Dublin, Alexander married Agnes Mayhew, the England-born daughter of Charles Mayhew Esq. They produced four children: Edith (id. 7.009), born in 1878; Lionel (id. 7.010), in 1880; Lyulph Frederick (id. 7.013), in 1883: and Florence (id. 7.016), in 1884. Lyulph is an old English name, combining ancient forms of the words 'flame' and 'wolf'. Interestingly, Frederick Pilkington, in his will, repeatedly referred to his grandson as Lyeth. Alexander, who also had property at Westbury, Stillorgan, died at Haggard House, Carbury, in 1887, aged forty, and was interred in the local churchyard. A note written on the only known photograph of him (see Figure 13) states 'Franco Prussian War 1870-1871' and shows him in ceremonial uniform. It is believed the garb was for a fancy-dress event.

Figure 13: Alexander Pilkington

The 1901 Irish Census indicates Agnes and three of her offspring residing at 145 Dartmouth Square, Rathmines and Rathgar East, Dublin. Agnes described both herself and her elder daughter Edith as ladies. Lyulph Frederick was identified as a gentleman and Florence as a scholar. Lionel was absent. He had assumed a military career and was engaged in the Boer War in South Africa, achieving the rank of lieutenant of the Royal Dublin Fusiliers, effectively a regiment of the British Army. He also was associated with the Royal Irish Rifles. In 1911, at which time the census recorded Lionel's residential address as 28.1 Merrion Street Upper, South Dock, Dublin, he sold Newberry Hall to the Robinson family for £8500. His grandfather Frederick Pilkington had bequeathed £20,000 to Lionel provided he did not marry until the age of thirty-six. For reasons not currently known, Lionel relocated to Australia in 1913. He departed from Liverpool on 22 April of that year on the White Star Line's *Medic*, in a fifty-six day journey to Melbourne. On 5 May 1916, barely a month after his thirty-sixth birthday, he married Bertha Harriet Maud Stephens, daughter of James Stephens and Elizabeth Burgess, in Launceston, Tasmania. In 1918, their only child Joyce Eileen was born. The voters' rolls for the period 1919 to 1928 list Lionel residing at 44 Balfour Street, Launceston, and then at 128 St John Street, Launceston until 1936. The rolls for this whole period show him as not employed and thus truly, he was a gentleman. He then disappeared from the roll, most likely returning to Ireland permanently after separating from wife and daughter. Lionel probably had earlier visited Ireland, as he is also recorded as having travelled from Liverpool to Melbourne on White Star Line's *Suevic*, commencing 9 April 1921. Lionel, who became master of the Edenderry Harriers, died in 1967 at St Kevin's Hospital, Dublin. His death certificate records his final residential address as 112 Dowland Road, Walkinstown.

Following the outbreak of war in the Pacific, daughter Joyce Eileen enlisted on 26 August 1942 at Melbourne in the Royal Australian Air Force as a NCO, Service Number 104129. Her rank until discharge on 23 January 1946 was aircraftwoman. She and her mother were registered on the voters' roll of 1943 as living at 18 The Righi, Heidelberg (now Eaglemont), Victoria, both listed as 'home duties', which probably was Joyce's address and role before enlistment. It is understood that she eventually migrated to the USA. Lionel's estranged wife Bertha died at Ivanhoe, Victoria in 1962, aged seventy-four.

Frances Ball Pilkington (id. 6.003)

The second daughter of Margaret and Frederick was born circa 1848 and known forever as Fanny. She married John Hornidge Esq., the son of George James Hornidge Esq., in 1872 at St George's Church, Dublin. Immediately prior to their marriage, Fanny had lived with her parents at 8 Rutland Square East, Dublin, and John had lived at the family home Calverston, near Mullingar, County Westmeath. Together, they produced four children: Sybil Pilkington (id. 7.004), born in 1873; Olive Hilda Beatrice Pilkington (id. 7.008), in 1877; Dudley George Pilkington (id. 7.012), in 1881: and Guy Mulock Pilkington (id. 7.015), in 1884. Interestingly, the Carbury Church baptisms of the first two state that the family lived at Haggard at the time. John Hornidge died at Mullingar in 1902. Fanny lived at 5.4 Mulgrave Terrace, Kingstown #2, Dublin, at the time of the 1911 Census and died in 1923 in Dublin.

Sybil did not marry and died in 1957. Olive married twice, the first time in 1903, but died without issue. Dudley studied at Pembroke College, Cambridge, England. Later in life, in addition to running a farm near Mullingar, he became a J.P. and a temporary lieutenant and acting captain of the local Royal Army Service Corps. He married Kathleen Harden, who produced two sons, John Dudley and Denis Richard, and a daughter, Pamela Marjery, as discussed below. The 1911 Irish Census indicates Dudley and family lived at #1 Calverstown, Clonfad, Mullingar, County Westmeath, which is also recorded in the 1958 edition of Burke's *The Landed Gentry of Ireland* as being the family seat. Dudley died in 1954, surviving his wife by eight years.

As mentioned earlier, communication between the descendants of Margaret Pilkington (nee Thom) and those of her brothers ceased towards the end of the nineteenth century, following the death of the family patriarch, Alex Thom. I am pleased to report that this silence has been broken after more than 120 years. Through contacts at Carbury, Kildare, during a visit in 2011, I met John Dudley's widow, Helen Lorraine, and Gail, third of her four daughters, both of whom now live in Cambridge, England, and are shown in Figure 14. John Dudley and Helen Lorraine had lived at Lockhouse 29 on the Royal Canal near Mullingar, and he had drowned in the canal in 1990, aged eighty. Details of the Hornidge family tree spanning from the 1500s to the late twentieth century and held by Helen Lorraine have been incorporated into the greater Pilkington family tree included in this book. I have since made contact also with now-Australia-based Deirdre Lidderdale (Schahinger), the eldest daughter of Denis Richard. Whilst both of my new-found Hornidge contacts were able to provide information on their streams of the Pilkington branch, they were unable to assist with information on the descendants of Fanny's siblings.

Figure 14: Lorraine Hornidge and Gail Jenner

Frederick Coddington Pilkington (id. 6.004)

Frederick Coddington, the second son of Margaret and Frederick, was born in 1849.

In 1872, he married Margaret Louisa Wilson, the second daughter of Joseph Wilson D.L., of Lissidian, County Armagh and of Westbury, Stillorgan. Wilson's great-grandfather had been appointed by American President George Washington as the country's Consul in Dublin, and his father was appointed by President John Quincy Adams to the same role. Frederick Coddington and Margaret, whose family home was at Stillorgan, Dublin, also had a city property, 30 Upper Merrion Street. Their first child, Frederick Ernest Chomley (id. 7.005), was born in 1873 and baptised at St Stephens Church on 5 January 1874. When their second child, Mina Olive (id. 7.007), was born in 1877, they lived at 28 Fitzwilliam Square. Frederick joined the Statistical and Social Inquiry Society of Ireland on 30 November 1880; that would have made his grandfather Alex proud. Frederick's son, a member of the Eighteenth Hussars, was killed at Waterval near Vryheid, South Africa, on 6 October 1901, fighting the Boers. He was unmarried. The 1901 Census return shows Frederick, his wife, and unmarried daughter Olive residing at House 1, Kilmacud East, Stillorgan, Dublin. Frederick described himself as a director of the Bank of Ireland. Research continues on Olive and descendants, if any.

The self-promotional publication *Progress in Irish Printing* issued in 1936 by Alex Thom and Co. Ltd. states that in 1890, Frederick Coddington Pilkington floated the business as a public limited company. As a man with extensive business and community activities including being a J.P., he retired from the company in 1903 and became Governor of the Bank of Ireland. In 1905, he was appointed a Commissioner of Charitable Donations and Bequests for Ireland and held that role for many years. He also was a member of the Constitutional Club, Northumberland Avenue, London, and a director of Great Southern and Western Railways, Ireland, when he died of influenza and a subsequent heart attack in 1924 at the Great Central Hotel, Marylebone, London. Probate was lodged in London on 4 April of that year to George Robert Deverell, the accountant-general of the Bank of Ireland, to his brother-in-law Major Joseph Reginald Wilson of HM Army, and to Nina Florence Wilson, spinster (possibly a sister-in-law). His effects were valued at £8359.8s.1d.

Maria Pilkington (id. 6.005)

Little is known of Maria. She was a minor beneficiary of her father's will. The protective nature of the wording used by Frederick in that document suggests that Maria, who was unmarried, might have been intellectually-challenged. He empowered his trustees to handle Maria's finances if they did not consider her competent enough to do so herself, and to determine with which of her sisters she should reside. Further, no mention is made of Maria in Harland's *History and Pedigrees of the Pilkingtons*, even though it well documents the details of her five sisters and the families into which they married.

Olivia Wade Pilkington (id. 6.006)

Olivia, the fourth daughter of Margaret and Frederick, was born in circa 1853. She married Scrope Bernard Christopher Rynd, Esq., the son of surgeon Dr Francis Rynd, at St George's Church, Dublin, in 1875. Prior to marriage, Olivia had resided with her parents at 8 Rutland Square East; Scrope had lived at 2 Upper Ely Place. The 1901 Irish Census recorded their home address as 1 Gortmore, Noughaval, County Westmeath, and his rank as J.P. The Gortmore property was a farm, as the will of his father-in-law Frederick, referred to loans made to him to stock it. Olivia and Scrope had no family. Scrope died in 1907 at Ballymahon, County Longford. The 1911 Irish Census recorded Olivia living at 28 Elgin Road, Pembroke West, Dublin, and identified her as a widow. Another resident in the home that night was her sister Maria. A notation applicable to both was 'income derived from land and interest on money'. It is not known when Olivia died or where she is buried.

Hamlet Wade Pilkington (id. 6.007)

Hamlet, the third son of Margaret and Frederick, was born in 1854. He was listed in newspaper reports as an attendee of the funeral service of his grandfather, Alex Thom the printer, in 1879. He never married and died in 1886, aged thirty-two. He is buried at Carbury Church.

William Handcock Pilkington (id. 6.008)

Frederick and Margaret's fourth son married Kathleen Richardson of 6 Albert Park, Liverpool, the daughter of the late Charles Mervyn Richardson, cotton broker, and Maria Louisa (nee Fosbery) of Cheshire, England, in 1887. The ceremony was at Christ Church, Sefton Park, in the parish of Walton-on-the-Hill, Lancashire. They had one child, Frederick Mervyn Fosbery Pilkington (id. 7.019), born in 1888. At Mervyn's baptism in Carbury Church, the family home was recorded as Ballyhagan House, opposite the entrance gates to Newberry Hall. At the time of the 1901 Irish Census, the family home was recorded as Haggard, though it would seem that the legal owner of this property was William's father Frederick, according to Clause 20 of the latter's will. William, formerly a lieutenant in the West York Militia, was knighted in 1904 for service to the community; he already was a J.P. and magistrate in Kildare, and in that year became High Sheriff. He died the following year and is buried in the grounds of Carbury Church. Interestingly, the church burial record shows his home as Ballyhagan House again. His wife survived him by fifty-two years, dying aged ninety, in England.

Mervyn attended a Church of England preparatory school in Wales as a boarder, as recorded in the 1901 Wales Census, and later attended Trinity College, Cambridge (B. A. 1910, M. A. 1913).

His address in the 1911 Census was Grosvenor Road, Richmond Surrey, where he lived with his mother. In 1914, he married Bertha Charlotte Georgina Bryan, the elder daughter of Loftus Anthony Bryan Esq., of Borrmouut Manor, Upton House, and Kilgibbon House, County Wexford. Mervyn served in France in World War I from 17 November 1915 as a captain in the Royal Army Service Corps, Special Reserve. Meanwhile, Bertha departed Liverpool on the St Louis, arriving at New York on 24 April 1916. She returned on the *Adriatic*, arriving at Southampton on 23 August 1919. The marriage ended the following year.

Mervyn, a member of the British Red Cross Society and The Order of St John of Jerusalem, remarried in 1925 at St George's, Hanover Square, London. His second wife was Ursula Marian Oxenford. He died in 1940 in Middlesex, and she in 1994, in Surrey. Research continues on establishing if they had any family; a note added in the distant past to the family tree in the sighted copy of Harland's *History and Pedigrees of the Pilkingtons* suggests they did not.

Edward Shenton Pilkington (id. 6.009)

Edward, the youngest son of Margaret and Frederick, was born circa 1861. He was a witness to the marriage of his brother William in 1887. His father bequeathed farmland at Rathbody and £9000 cash to him in 1898. Given the connection between farmers and their land, particularly land passed down through the generations, the general expectation would have been that he'd continue there, but he does not appear in the 1901 Irish Census. The next record of him after his father's death is on the 1909 electoral roll for the city of Ballarat, Victoria, Australia. It is not known when he migrated to The Antipodes. Edward probably headed to Ballarat in the knowledge that four of his paternal uncles, Joseph, William, Hamlet and Robert Pilkington, and their sister Fanny, had settled there from Ireland more than fifty years earlier.

Edward died unmarried on 14 May 1912 at 98 Myers Street, Geelong, Victoria, aged fifty-one. Why he moved to Geelong is uncertain; Robert Thom, a maternal uncle, had settled there forty years earlier but had died in the 1890s, and his surviving family had largely left the region by 1910. Edward's estate, valued for probate at £4495, included a 542-acre farm at Karramomus in northern Victoria valued at £3383, and £1002 in the Commercial Bank at Shepparton. It is not clear if Edward ever worked the land, as there was no livestock or crop on it and no machinery included in his assets.

Evidence suggests that Edward was ill for some time before his death. His last will dated 20 February 1912 was witnessed by a live-in nurse, and a medical doctor's bill settled from his estate was substantial. His last residence and place of death was adjacent to a hospital and quite possibly was a hospice. He is buried in the Church of England section of East Geelong Cemetery. The sole beneficiary of Edward's will was R. R. Affleck, whose identity initially was not known to me. Additionally, the executors of the will settled a debt of £30 to F. M. Affleck 'for board'. This prompted further research, and the story is continued in the section devoted to the Australian Pilkingtons later in this chapter.

Eveline Maud Pilkington (id. 6.010)

Known as Maud, the tenth child and fifth daughter of Margaret and Frederick was born in Carbury in circa 1862, well before the purchase of Newberry Hall. This leads to the conclusion that Margaret and Frederick were spending at least some of their time at Haggard. When as a minor Maud married John Charles Lyons Esq. J.P., at the Church of St Stephen, Dublin, in 1882, she gave her address as Newberry Hall. Lyons, born and still then living in Ledestown, County Westmeath, was the son of another John Charles Lyons Esq., D.L. The younger John became High Sheriff for that area in 1883, in which year a son, John Charles Geoffrey Pilkington (id. 7.014), was born, followed over the next six years by two daughters, Gladys Maude Pilkington (id. 7.018) and Coral Cecil Constance (id. 7.020).

The 1901 Irish Census records the family home as 2 Williamstown, Kilrainey, County Kildare, with Maud as head of family of the two daughters, then both scholars. Maud stated that she was married and in receipt of an annuity (as verified in her father's will). It is not known whether the description, head of family, was an administrative requirement of the census process in the temporary absence of her husband from the family home, or whether Maud and her husband had separated. John Lyons died in 1908.

By the time of the 1911 Census, Maud and her daughters had relocated to 2 Ledestown, Hopestown, County Westmeath. Maud described herself as a widow and both daughters as single. In that same census, a Geoffrey Lyons, twenty-seven, retired Army officer and single, was residing at 49.2 York Road, Kingstown #3, Dublin. It is believed but not yet confirmed that he was Maud's son. Research continues on all three siblings.

Violet Josephine Pilkington (id. 6.011)
The youngest child of Margaret and Frederick was born in 1864. As a twenty-year-old, she married Huband George Gregg Esq., J.P.

in 1885, at the Church of St Stephen, Dublin. Gregg was the son of Francis Thornton Gregg, a clerk in Holy Orders, and lived at Oldtown, Edgeworthstown, County Longford. He was seventeen years Violet's senior, had been married before, had become father to a boy Thornton Huband who died in infancy in 1875, and had lost his wife Jessie, in 1881. Huband and Violet had four children: William Thornton Huband (id. 7.017), born in 1886; Hamlet Pilkington Huband (id. 7.021), in 1890; Violet Pilkington Huband (id. 7.022), in 1893, and Joseph (id. 7.026), in 1900. Joseph died in infancy.

The 1901 Irish Census recorded the family residence as 6 Kilmacud East, Stillorgan, Dublin. Huband was identified as a land agent. Coincidentally, the census recorded Violet's niece, Olive Hornidge, as an overnight guest. Son William was recorded in the England and Wales Census on the same day as a boarder at a school in Preshute Parish, Marlborough, Wiltshire, whilst son Hamlet was recorded as a boarder at a school in Llanddulas Parish, County Denbighshire, Wales. The 1911 Irish Census recorded the family living at the same Stillorgan address. Huband described himself as railway director. Research continues on the descendants of the three surviving siblings, all of whom married. The 1958 edition of Burke's *The Landed Gentry of Ireland*, from which much of the family tree data was extracted, records Ballyknockane House, Ballypatrick, Clonmel, Tipperary, as being the Gregg family seat.

Newberry Hall

Newberry Hall, the Pilkington family home, is a most imposing residence in Carbury, located fifty-two kilometres west of Dublin.

The village is named after Carbury Castle, the ruins of which sit high on a hill overlooking it. The village, which in former days also carried the alternative name of Castle Carbury, was small. In 1894, the parish of 4796 acres had a population of 340, and the 671 acres of townlands had a population of 63.

Newberry Hall is a Palladian-style home of significant merit and importance, surrounded originally by 588 acres of fine limestone farming land. It is a three-storey brick structure with stone dressings. The main kitchen is in the basement. Nine bedrooms and the living rooms occupy the two main floors. The house is flanked by two pavilions, one for the steward of the estate, the other housing the stables, the coach house, and workers' quarters. Adjacent to the house is a three-acre walled garden which includes glasshouses and a pond.

Researcher James Robinson in a paper on the property wrote that the home was designed by Nathaniel Clements and built in the 1760s for Arthur Pomeroy, later known as Lord Haberton. It was originally called Newberry. In 1747, Pomeroy married Mary Colley of Carbury Castle, thus obtaining the title to the Newberry land. The house had unrestricted views to the castle. The land of Newberry had flax holes for the processing of its crop. An ice house on the estate was used to store ice taken from the pond in wintertime to preserve food for the house. The property remained within the Pomeroy/Haberton family through a number of generations, being leased at times to outsiders. In 1850, the rated value of the property was £485.15s. In about 1851, it was sold to Edward Breton Wolstenholme, who renamed it Newberry Hall. Around 1870, the property was purchased by Frederick and Margaret Pilkington.

Minor renovations were carried out in the 1880s, with both running water throughout the house and a tennis court being added. A second court was added a decade later; otherwise, the property is essentially as originally built. Adjoining the tennis courts is a large weeping beech tree grafted upside down on to another beech tree, the work of a gardener named Stapleton. It is said there was a small paper mill on the property, which is understandable considering Frederick's printing, publishing, and bookbinding business interests.

The Pilkington family owned Newberry Hall for over forty years (though various genealogical research sites say that at least some of the Pilkington children were born there, meaning ownership somewhat earlier than 1870) until it was sold in 1911 to Richard Robinson. Newberry Hall Demesne, now reduced to 444 acres, remained within the Robinson family for ninety-nine years, until it was purchased by a neighbouring farmer, who is restoring it to its former glory. The advertised price was 7.5 million euros. Figure 15 is from the advertising literature.

Figure 15: Newberry Hall

The property is steeped in history. The avenue approaching the home crosses an ancient stone bridge close to Trinity Well, which has been a place of pilgrimage from early Christian times and being recorded as early as 1305. Pilgrims still attend on Trinity Sunday each year. Trinity Well is also significant in that it is the source of the River Boyne. In the 1798 Rising, Newberry was attacked by insurrectionists after the Battle of Clonard on 11 July. They took over the property, looted the house, made short work of the booze in the cellar, and took four guineas from Lord Haberton's desk, together with four horses and the clothes of the lord's estate agent, Brian Forde. They then murdered two sisters, dairymaids Mary and Esther Grattan, who were the only Protestants employed on the estate. One of the sisters was shot, the other drowned in Newberry pond close to the main entrance. A year later, four men were convicted of the murders and condemned to be hanged beside the same pond. One of them escaped from custody by dressing as a woman, so cheating the gallows.

Carbury's Church of Ireland

In the nineteenth century, religion played a major part in societal life, and the local church was the focal point, particularly for those who lived in and around small villages such as Carbury. Many members of the Pilkington extended family, and even the Dublin-based first two grandchildren of Margaret and Frederick, were christened in the Carbury Church of Ireland, and a number of them are buried in the grounds surrounding it. To some, it provided an opportunity to memorialise their loved ones.

The loss of his wife earlier, and then of two sons during the 1880s, moved Frederick Pilkington to memorialise them all in a stained glass window behind the altar (see Figure 16). It is inscribed: 'To the Glory of God and in Memory of Margaret the Wife and Alexander and Hamlet Wade two of the Sons of Frederick Pilkington by whom this window was erected 1891'.

Figure 16: Carbury Church of Ireland Window

On the pulpit is another dedication: 'To the Glory of God. Built in Memory of Alexander Pilkington, born Sept 30th 1846, Died March 10th 1887. Erected by his Widow'.

On the Holy Communion table, a brass plaque reads: 'To the Glory of God and sacred to the Memory of May, granddaughter of Frederick Pilkington Esq. of Newberry Hall, and dearly beloved Wife of Lieut.-Colonel W. H. E. Woodwright of The Grove, Branksome Park, who fell asleep on the 19th March 1928 at Bournemouth. This

Holy Communion table is presented by her sorrowing husband to the church she loved'.

Two matching brass plaques erected in 1908 by Mrs Alex Pilkington are dedicated to the Glory of God, and in loving memory of her sister Marian Maudslay, and of her two brothers Ernest Mayhew and Colonel C. C. Mayhew, respectively.

In the church grounds are five graves relating to the greater Pilkington family.

On the headstone of a single grave, the inscription reads:

'This stone has been placed here by Frederick Pilkington of Newberry Hall as a small token of affection and esteem and to mark the place where are interred the mortal remains of his uncle, the Rev'd William Coddington who died 26th of May 1867'.

On the headstone of another single grave, the inscription reads:

'Here lie the mortal remains of Hamlet Wade Pilkington, Third and Most Dearly-Beloved Son of Frederick Pilkington of Newberry Hall. He died 10th Nov 1886, aged 32 years'.

The inscription on a third single grave reads:

'In Loving Memory of Sir William Handcock Pilkington. Died June 23, 1905. Aged 45'.

On the first of two joint gravesites, matching headstones read:

'This Stone was erected here by Frederick Pilkington of Newberry Hall, to mark the spot wherein lie the mortal remains of his Dearly Beloved Wife Margaret, who died 23rd Aug 1878, aged 53 years'.

'In Loving Memory of Frederick Pilkington of Newberry Hall. Died May 19th, 1898, aged 79 years'.

On the other joint gravesite, are two inscriptions:

'In Memory of a Loving Husband and Father, Alexander Pilkington, who died March 10, 1887, aged 42. Thy will be done'.

'Also of a Loving Wife and Mother, Agnes Pilkington, died 14th Feb 1925. Now the labourer's work is done'.

Carbury Church still has services, but they are nowhere near as often as in days gone by. A row of stables is located opposite the church to provide shelter for the worshippers' horses during service in the winter months. The stables were last used decades ago but remain as a visual reminder of life in former days.

The Australian Pilkingtons

This sub-section is at the writer's indulgence and is included for several reasons. Ballarat, situated in central Victoria, became the adopted home in the mid-1800s for five of the six siblings of Frederick Pilkington, and for Frederick's son Edward in the early 1900s; the writer grew up an hour's drive from Ballarat and was married there; and Victoria has by far the greatest concentration of Thom family descendants anywhere in the world, all the descendants of Robert. There was, of course, no blood connection between the early Pilkington immigrants and Robert's family, nor is there any knowledge of social contact between the two groups.

The book *Harland's History and Pedigrees of the Pilkingtons* referred to earlier states that the Reverend Joseph Pillkington of County Tyrone, Ireland, had six sons, one of whom, Frederick Pilkington, married Margaret Thom. The book's family tree (Sheet 9) differs slightly from its text, showing the reverend's offspring to be five sons and one daughter as below:

Joseph died at Melbourne about 1865 d.s.p. (ie. without issue).

Hamlet, living in Victoria, 1853, had several children.

William, d.s.p.

Fanny was the wife of Morton, Ballarat.

Frederick married Margaret Thom (etc).

Richard, of Farbane, Kings Co. (See Will 1842. d.s.p.)

The family tree did not mention the youngest son Robert, or that both he and William also had migrated to Australia.

Gold was discovered near Ballarat (originally spelt Ballaarat), in August 1851. Within a month, 1,000 miners were on site, and by 1853, an estimated 20,000 miners were trying their luck. It is easy to assume the Pilkington brothers and their sister were part of that massive migration. However, the possibility also exists that the Great Famine (also called the Irish Potato Famine) of 1845-52, during which time one million people died and another million emigrated from Ireland, might have been the trigger for their move to Australia. Immigration records do not reveal when or how they travelled to Victoria, either individually or as a group, but circumstantial evidence suggests they probably were in the country before the discovery of gold at Ballarat.

Voters' rolls for 1856 list Joseph, William, Hamlet and Robert Pilkington all as gentlemen farmers and owners of freehold property at Talangatta in the Warrnambool Heytesbury district in south western Victoria. The same four are also listed at the same time as being timber merchants in Japan Street, Warrnambool, at a property owned by a Mr Davidson. Whilst the voters' rolls are not in themselves proof they were the brothers of Frederick, there is a high statistical probability that they were.

Joseph Pilkington died in 1862 in Victoria, aged thirty-nine years (Victorian Death Index, Registration No. 7136).

William Pilkington died at Geelong on 8 September 1867 of gunshot wounds accidentally received (Reg'n 8336). *The Argus* newspaper of 21 September 1867 reported he was born in County Tyrone, Ireland, the second son of the late Rector Joseph Pilkington, and died aged forty-nine. The death notice did not mention if he was married or had children. The subsequent inquest is filed in Reg'n 628.

Hamlet Pilkington remains a mystery, suggesting he may have had additional given names used only at birth, marriage, and death.

Frances (Fanny) Pilkington married George Glenwilliam Morton at Warrnambool in 1853 (Reg'ns 629 and 31903). Fanny lived to seventy-five and died at Ballarat in 1900 (Reg'n 257). George died at home one year later, also aged seventy-five (Reg'n 6252). There were four offspring from the marriage, as below.

The first child, Frances Mary, was born at Labona, the family property at Learmonth near Ballarat in 1856 (Reg'n 8259). An 1895 photograph of the property and its family is shown on the Museum Victoria website. Frances married James Philip MacPherson in 1880 (Reg'n 1487). He died at West Melbourne in 1891, aged forty-nine (Reg'n 11640). Her second husband, Robert Rutherford Affleck, was born at Aspley in 1863 (Reg'n 20753). They married at Horsham in 1892 (Reg'n 5077) and had one child, Robert Morton Affleck, born at Ballarat in 1893 (Reg'n 28454). It was Frances who was recompensed £30 from the estate of her cousin Edward Shenton Pilkington for an outstanding debt for board, and Robert Rutherford Affleck was the sole beneficiary of Edward's will. Why Edward specified his cousin's husband rather than his cousin herself is not known. Frances died on 24 November 1915 at her home, Hawthorne House, Mangara Road Canterbury, in Melbourne, aged fifty-nine. A death notice in *The Argus* newspaper the following day stated she was a granddaughter of the late Reverend Joseph Pilkington, chaplain to Sir Thomas Hardy's fleet in the Battle of Trafalgar and then chaplain at the British Embassy in Madrid, which data aligns with that of Harland's book. Her husband, Robert, lived for another twenty-six years, dying at Balwyn, aged seventy-eight.

The second child, George Morton, was born in 1859 on the family farm (Reg'n 2695). He died fourteen days later (Reg'n 1561).

The third child, Georgina Anne (Gina), was born at Burrumbeet near Learmonth in 1860 (Reg'n 19903). In 1893, she married James Guthrie Affleck, younger brother of her brother-in-law Robert Rutherford Affleck (Reg'n 998). James was born at

Edenhope in 1867 (Reg'n 8010). There were no children from the marriage. James died 13 January 1904 (Reg'n 189) and was buried in Ballarat's Old Cemetery. Gina died 23 April 1910 at her residence, Opawa, Wendouree Parade Ballarat, aged forty-nine, and was buried in the same cemetery. She bequeathed her estate to her cousin Edward Shenton Pilkington, who was residing with her at the time. He received a cheque for £914.18.0d.

The fourth child, Frederick, died eight days after birth in 1862 at Burrumbeet (Reg'n 1872).

As reported in *The Argus* newspaper the following day, Robert, the youngest son of the late Reverend Joseph Pilkington, married Emily Eliza Thomas on 5 August 1852 by special licence at Trinity Church, Pentridge (now Coburg), in Melbourne. Emily was the youngest daughter of William Thomas Esq., J.P., guardian of Aborigines, Strangway, Pentridge. Robert died in 1883, aged fifty-three (Reg'n 8197). Emily died in 1897 at North Fitzroy (Reg'n 8751) after producing twelve offspring, as below.

An unnamed girl was born and died at birth in Warrnambool in 1855 (Reg'n 2038).

Robert Hamlet was born at Collingwood in 1857 (Reg'n 8380). He married Caroline Elizabeth Mc Kenzie in 1888 (Reg'n 5389). He possibly died at Kew in 1897 (Reg'n 9359).

Sarah Susannah was born at Merrick in 1859 (Reg'n 266). She married Henry William Champion at Fitzroy in 1898 (Reg'n 5748).

Frederick was born in 1860 (Reg'n 453) and died fourteen days later, possibly at Northcote (Reg'n 293).

Frances Edith was born in 1861 (Reg'n 6799) at Sandridge (now Port Melbourne) and died there two years later (Reg'n 4945).

John Pascoe was born at Brunswick in 1862 (Reg'n 20103).

Frederick Herbert, born 1863, died at Brunswick two years later (Reg'n 3630).

Frances Elizabeth was born at Collingwood in 1864 (Reg'n 21135).

Georgina Margaret was born at Brunswick in 1866 (Reg'n 13331) and died in 1868, aged two (Reg'n 3296).

Olivia was born at Brunswick in 1868 (Reg'n 1146) and married David Thomson at Northcote in 1897 (Reg'n 6693).

Hamlet Wade (possibly Robert Hamlet Wade) was born in 1868 at Brunswick (Reg'n 21851) and married Fran Emily Dykes in 1900 (Reg'n 373).

Edward was born at Brunswick in 1869 (Reg'n 20878) and died three weeks later in 1870 (Reg'n 507).

In summary, from the five siblings of Frederick Pilkington who migrated to Australia, there are seven family streams whose descendants probably still live here; those of Robert Morton Affleck and the six mature offspring of Robert Pilkington. This incomplete data is included for interest only, as the members of this group are not blood descendants of the 'original' Alexander Thom. However, it may be of assistance at some time in the future to researchers of the Pilkington family. All of the places mentioned are in Victoria.

CHAPTER 7

WALTER OF CULLEN

This chapter relates to Walter Thom (id. 5.007), the seventh child of Alex and Maria and the second of three sons to continue the family line.

Walter was born in May 1835. Family lore has it that Walter had little interest in his father's printing business; his interest lay in farming. Alex did not want Walter to adopt the habits of his younger brother Robert, whose sole involvement in the printing firm was a brief daily visit to the office to raid the petty cash box to support his active social life of long and lavish lunches. He arranged for Walter a resident studentship with John Bolton, who ran a 300-acre farm, Cullen, at Beauparc, County Meath, about twenty-eight miles from Dublin. Cullen originally was part of the Conyngham Estate of Slane Castle before being purchased by the Bolton family in 1790.

Walter's studentship at Cullen was formalised in a contract which spelt out his duties and the conditions of employment for the next thirty months. The contract was 'for the purpose of acquiring a knowledge of farming and becoming conversant with all matters connected with agricultural pursuits'. It was signed by Alex, Walter, John Bolton, and two witnesses on 3 March 1855. The full agreement is shown as Appendix 14. The wording was formal but still sufficiently loose to allow Walter to fall for his master's second daughter, Mary Ann Ruxton Bolton (id. 5.007A), a strapping young lady reportedly over six feet tall, whom he married in 1864 at St Thomas Church in Dublin. They established home in Dublin, in the comfort of Donnycarney House.

Over the next thirteen years, Walter and Mary Ann had ten children: Alexander (id. 6.012), born in 1865; Walter (id. 6.013), in 1866; Dillon Turner (id. 6.014), in 1868; Maria Victoria Elizabeth (id. 6.016), in 1869; Robert (id. 6.017), in circa 1870; Sarah (id. 6.018), in 1871; John Bolton Ruxton (id. 6.020), in 1873; Frederick Pilkington (id. 6.021), in 1874; Hubert Ernest (id. 6.023), in 1875; and Frederick Robert (id. 6.025), in 1877. The family tree is shown as Appendix 17. During this time, Walter's mother Maria died, and his father remarried. The return of now-stepmother Sarah to Donnycarney House prompted Walter and family to move to Hollybrook Park, Clontarf. A photo of Walter from circa 1872 is shown as Figure 17. Walter and family later moved to 16 Garville Avenue, Rathgar, according to *Thom's Dublin Directory* of 1881.

Figure 17: Walter Thom

By then, looking after Cullen was beyond Mary Ann's father, who passed it over to her and Walter to manage and, in the process, to look after him. In the words of Mary Ann's granddaughter, Sally Henderson, in 1987:

I gathered that she (Mary Ann) did this, but the poor old man's life was a bit of a misery. Of course, she was most difficult in every way. Walter was quiet and easy-going, and she ruled the roost. The old man used to be shut up at times in the front hall here, and there are to this day, the marks of his stick on the pitch pine wood of the door. He died in 1900 and is buried in Slane. The story was that he wished to be buried with his wife (possibly at Bective in County Meath or Castlering in County Louth, I can't recall which), but Mary Ann decided he would be buried in Slane, which was close by and convenient.

Walter and Mary Ann continued to operate Cullen. They also had bought a farm at nearby Knowth, bordering the Boyne River and adjacent to the Newgrange neolithic passage tombs for their son Alexander to work. The farm comprised 180 acres of prime land and had a five-bedroom home with three reception rooms and servants' quarters. Alexander went his own way after a trial period there, and the farm was auctioned on 24 November 1893. The advertising literature stated that a fair rent for the property was £210 per annum.

Walter, the last surviving son of Alex, died in 1909 and is buried in the family vault at Mt. Jerome. Mary Ann stayed on at Cullen until 1920, when she decided to move to Reynella, a home in County Westmeath, which she had passed to Frederick, her youngest son. She shared the house with him until her death the following year. She is buried with her husband. Family lore has it that there were problems in fitting her over-length coffin into the vault, leading someone to say she was 'difficult in life, difficult in death'. Nonetheless, she showed a compassionate side in her will, perhaps in recognition of the fact that her brother-in-law Robert had died virtually destitute in Australia. Of her total estate value of £16,640, Mary Ann bequeathed £250 to both William and Fanny, and £100 to Mabel, the three surviving progeny of Robert. Of Walter and Mary Ann's ten children, eight died without family, as told below.

Walter Thom (id. 6.013)

Walter, the second child, died in his twentieth year, at 9 o'clock on a bright fine morning of 1886, according to an inscription in a family Bible originally given to his father in 1850, passed to Walter, and on his death, passed to his brother Dillon Turner. Walter never married. He is buried in the family vault at Mt. Jerome. The polished oak coffin with solid brass mountings, together with the burial service fees, cost £39.15s.

Maria Victoria Elizabeth Thom (id. 6.016)

Maria, the fourth child, was the elder of only two daughters. The first ten years of her life were in Dublin, before the family moved to Cullen. She was very much under the control of her mother, and it was widely accepted she had a miserable and a lonely life. Figure 18 shows her as a young woman. Her elder brothers wanted her to go abroad just as they had, but she wouldn't consider it; in those days, it would have been a big step for a young woman to take.

Figure 18: Maria Victoria Elizabeth Thom, circa 1887

In 1909, she was bequeathed an annuity of only £25 of her father's £37,000 estate, her mother being the main beneficiary. Maria contested the will in court and was successful in having the annuity increased to £80 and to £200 after her mother's death. Nonetheless, Maria still faced financial problems and was unsettled. Occasionally, she went up to Dublin to stay with her brother Dillon Turner and family at Kimberley, Cowper Road. During one such visit, she committed suicide. She was found in her bedroom one morning with her throat cut and a razor by her side. She was aged forty. Newspapers covering the subsequent inquest reported she had left a note lamenting her dire financial position and expressing concern about not being successful in her suicide attempt. In the words of her niece Sally Henderson:

The resultant scandal was enormous, and never talked about—typical of those times. My sympathy is so much with her, the only girl among all those boys. One would think she would have been adored.

Robert Thom (id. 6.017)

Robert, the fifth child, apparently was delicate and frail and suffered respiratory problems. His parents believed his condition was exacerbated by the cold air of Ireland, so they sent him to the more temperate climate of the Isle of Wight. In spite of this move, he reportedly died as a young man and is buried there.

Sarah Thom (id. 6.018)

Sarah died at the age of two. She is buried in the family vault at Mt. Jerome.

John Bolton Ruxton Thom (id. 6.020)

John, known as Jack, suffered the same poor health as Robert. He was sent to Jersey in the Channel Islands to relieve his condition, boarding at Victoria College. He died of blood poisoning at age seventeen and was buried four days later in an unmarked grave Q140 North in Newmont-A-L'abbe Cemetery, on a hilltop above the capital, St Helier. The total burial fee was £24. 2s. 6d.

Frederick Pilkington Thom (id. 6.021)

Frederick died as an infant, just two months old, in 1874. A newspaper reported that death was due to complications from a vaccination. He is buried at Mt. Jerome.

Hubert Ernest Thom (id. 6.023)

Hubert died one month after birth in 1875. He also is buried at Mt. Jerome. The cost of the burial service was £2. 2s. 6d.

Frederick Robert Thom (id. 6.025)

Frederick, the youngest child, lived to well past middle age but never married. He was a member of the Royal College of Physicians and the Royal College of Surgeons. He led a relatively comfortable life, having been bequeathed £8000 in his father's will. In 1914, he enlisted for the First World War and survived the conflict. On return, he moved to Reynella, the home that his mother had passed to him. As mentioned above, Mary Ann Ruxton, around 1920, went to live there with Frederick until her death the following year. Family lore has it that Mary Ann used to sit in her wheelchair on the landing at the top of the staircase and keep a sharp eye on all that was going on below. Another family story is that Frederick removed the roof from his barn in order to reduce his council taxes. Frederick, who at the time was living at another home he owned, Clonlost at Killucan, County Westmeath, died at the Greville Arms Hotel, Mullingar, in 1933.

Let us now follow the lives of the other two siblings: Alexander, and Dillon Turner, both of whom continued the family line and name into the seventh generation.

Alexander Thom (id. 6.012)

Alexander was the eldest of the ten children of Walter and Mary Ann; he was born in 1865. We are fortunate that in his eighties, Alexander put pen to paper and started to record life's memories. Regrettably, he never completed the task, but this in no way diminishes the value of his efforts.

My grandfather, Alexander Thom, drove in every morning to the printer's office at 87/88 Middle Abbey St., and my great delight was to join the coachman James Breslin on the box. He drove two horses named Bertie and Leck, which had been bought at Labouette's, who was a noted man in Dublin in those days. Many a time, Breslin drove the carriage into the sea along the Fairfield Road, where the Jardens are now, to clean the horses' legs on the way home in the morning.

Our house at Hollybrook Park was haunted, and as a child, I remember hearing the noises in the kitchen, with everyone listening upstairs. No servant would sleep below stairs, and we left the house in a year, going to 3 Zion Terrace, Rathgar, beside the Zion Church.

O'Connell's Centenary (of his birth, 6 August 1775) was a fine sight, with trade bands in procession down Grafton Street to College Green and fire brigades with their horses. There was an amnesty for everyone, I suppose, referring to the Fenian prisoners who were then in jail. I was on the steps of the Alliance offices, now the Northern Bank, and I saw it all.

I was in a window in Dame Street when the Lord Mayor's funeral passed through in 1872. The first flag was the flag of India, with a star in the centre. The tenantry went in front and then the troops. Sir John Gray's funeral in Glasnevin was a puzzle to me as a small boy. I kept asking why he as a Protestant wasn't buried at Mount Jerome and was told that he was a great friend of O'Connell and wanted to be buried beside him.

Nelson's Pillar was always there, but I saw Father Matthews' statue unveiled, then came Sir John Gray's. O'Connell's and Parnell's I found when I returned thirty years later, and Smith O'Brien had been moved from the junction of Westmoreland St. and Dolier St. to where it is now.

I trotted down Rathgar to school every morning for ten years, and most of the judges and lawyers walked to their courts and offices. Horse buses were running, but we never used them. I saw the first horse tram run up Rathgar Road and got a good licking from my father for putting a penny on the track to get it flattened. A school friend had his toe cut off doing the same trick.

During a visit to my maternal grandmother's home at Cullen House, County Meath, in the seventies, I saw Charles Stewart Parnell elected for Meath. He brought two bannerettes with him in procession, and I heard that his ancestors had brought them to Ireland with Strongbow. I heard him tell the 'men of Meath' that he would get them security of tenure, fair rents, and free sale, and that he would get the labourers a house and half an acre of land for one shilling a week. I often heard the labourers say they would never get the land, but Parnell got it through within five years.

The year 1879 was the first year of United States cattle coming to Ireland and our own slump in cattle prices.

Together with all of my brothers, I went to school in Dublin, until the family moved to Cullen in 1880. Then I was sent to Trent College near Nottingham for a year. I went to visit my Aunt Maria in London during the Easter holidays and saw all the sights. I went home for the summer holidays and made, or helped to make, twenty-three acres of hay for my father in Newtown, where he had taken the meadows from Pat Nulty. I left school at Christmas 1880 and have been learning ever since.

I went with father and brother Walter to the fair at Balla on 11 August 1881 and bought thirty-three longhorn bullocks from Pat Loole of Westport at £11.10s and £10.10s each. We walked them all the way home, and it took about nine or ten days, Brian Mc Cabe driving, not a bit footsore. These bullocks sold for £24 each during the following summer, the best profit I ever remember on cattle. I went to Balla again in 1882 and bought for £13, but they didn't do nearly as well. Billy Blake taught me to plough, and I spent hours with him holding a big beam plough swinging without wheels. Easy enough when you get the knack, but you have to learn it.

I probably saw the last farmers' show in Kildare Street and remember being there with Father when he showed me what he called the Polled Angus and told me they were the finest cattle in the world. He was right. I also remember the first show at Ballsbridge with King Edward VII, then Prince of Wales, and the Marquis of Lorn, afterwards Duke of Argyle. As a child with Father, I thought the cocked hats they wore, with white plumes, were a fine sight.

Dublin was very nervous over the Phoenix Park murders on 6 May 1882; police were everywhere. At the time, we had a lot of men helping with the hay-making, mostly strangers from Cavan. One man never drew his money. He went off one night after six or seven days' work, and it was only then that we thought he might have been hiding amongst the other men. Foot and mouth came in '83 and '85 and went through the country like wildfire. It was during the summer, and although we lost no cattle, they did lose a lot of condition.

My brother Walter, aged twenty, died on 4 January 1886, one year younger than myself. I missed him sadly; we would have made a great team in the cattle business.

The year 1887 was a bad year for the cattle trade, as Canadian animals were coming over in ever-increasing numbers. In 1888, I got tired of working for no pay and got a letter of introduction from Richard Kavanagh, the big betting man in Dublin in those days, to a man in Colorado, USA. I made up all the Cullen hay for Father and sailed on the SS *Egbert* for New York on 1 August. The whole city was in mourning for General Sheridan, who had just died; flags were at half mast everywhere.

I got my ticket to Denver and went across in a ferry to Jersey City, where I took the Lake Erie Express. At a place called Sholola

Glen in Pennsylvania, there had been a landslide which a freight train had run into, leaving the engine lying on its side right in our track. Our train, travelling at about 50mph, hit it and rolled into the Delaware River. The carriage I was in rolled over and over, 120 feet into the river on its side. I must have been unconscious for a bit but remember seeing the light of a fire shining on the river. I managed to scramble out and, with some other passengers, went up the river's edge to get away from the burning train which was on the slope over us. A little flat-bottomed boat came across with one man in it. He could only carry two in it, so we put the women in first, and afterwards, we all got over. Doctor Van Ettem patched me up, and the railway sent a train to take us to Port Jarvis, where I spent eight weeks in the hospital. Everyone was very kind; George Fairman especially took me out for drives and showed me the country when I was convalescing. I had two broken ribs, a badly wrenched back, and my head was dinged a bit. Mrs Lantry came to see me; she had lost eleven horses in the wreck and wanted me to go on with Abby, her manager, to Los Angeles, where she had a ranch. But I had had enough of America and came home on the *City of Chicago* to Cork.

I returned to work at Cullen. In 1889, Father bought land at Knowth for me, but he never gave it to me; I was only stopping in it. After a year, I gave it up to him and went to Australia, a fine country, working on the boat en route there. I had almost no money, but I did have the gold repeater watch that my grandfather had bequeathed me. I was prepared to sell the watch if necessary but managed to survive without resorting to that. I met my uncle Charles Bolton in Newcastle, New South Wales. He wanted me to stop in his house as long as I liked as a visitor, but I would not loaf at home. His daughter Mrs Geary was also very kind, but I wanted to get a job of work without depending on anyone.

After a week or so, I took a train to Brisbane, arriving in the evening. Next morning, I went looking for a job and asked a policeman on his beat if he knew where there was a registry office. I went in and asked for a job and was told I would have one in two days if I would pay a £1 fee. I refused to pay until I had the job. We compromised and I paid 2/6 down and the balance when I had the job. I then went to the Labour Bureau and met an Irishman named Brennan, gave him my name and told him I wanted a job. He said he knew my grandfather, Alexander Thom. He had an order to send up twenty men to Gore and Co. at Yandilla Station at once, to reap wheat at 15/—a week and food. I started next morning by train to Pittsworth Station and got there by sundown. I had taken my cabin trunk as far as Pittsworth, and I took out a spare shirt and a bag, strapped them on my back, left the trunk in the parcel office, and started to walk to Yandilla. I walked all night until I could not see anymore and then lay down under a tree to sleep. I woke up with the sun and carried on, finally coming across a Chinaman shepherd, who gave me some breakfast and pointed out the way to Yandilla. I got there at last, very tired. I met Frank Gore in the office, and he told me to go and get another breakfast. I rested for a bit and was then told to walk another seven miles to Sandridge, where the wheat was.

Some ruffians had come up with the others and, from the start, wanted to strike for higher wages. I heard them planning it one night at the fire. They said they would not make a move until the morning the wheat was ready to be cut. Four or five of us made up our minds that we would not go on strike, and on the morning they started, we turned out to work and kept one machine going. Frank Gore was sent for and rode out past where we were working. He must have seen us but didn't stop. He gave all the strikers everything they asked for and started them at midday. When the harvest was over, we got the same cheques as the strikers, but we were taken on permanently to work on the station and the strikers got the boot.

Yandilla was a station on the Darling Downs, with beautiful black alluvial soil which would grow anything. The downs ran along the banks of the Condamine River with plenty of trees and was an ideal place for stock of all kinds. I saw shorthorn bullocks, which must have been 17 or 18 cwt, above average weight. But Yandilla was a sheep station; I had to mind a ram which had cost £300 and had to see him every day. He was kept in a paddock of about 18 acres or so, and one of my jobs was to see him with 30 or 40 ewes. I believe Yandilla has now been subdivided to provide closer settlement and has reduced in size to a little over 6,000 acres round the homestead.

A human interest story in relation to Alexander's time at Yandilla, as recorded by Alexander's daughter Sally Henderson, is worth repeating here.

The Gores had a young family, and Dad used to take a small daughter in front of him on the saddle for rides close around the station. Many years later, early in 1930, as I remember, people called Target came to live close to us here. Mrs Target was an

Australian and heard Dad had been out there. They met and found she had been the little girl on the saddle. She remembered him well.

A Google search <Yandilla Station Queensland> revealed a wealth of information on the property. Yandilla, located 200 km west of Brisbane, covered 1789 sq km in the 1890s. Essentially, it was a small town with its own store, school, and telegraph station. Its primary interest was rearing sheep for wool. A portion of the land ultimately was sequestered by the state, and a town, now called Millmerran, was established on what is now known as the Gore Highway. Further Internet research led to a series of period photographs of Yandilla, held by the State Library of Queensland. They include a shearing shed scene and two group photos of the Gores with their young children. It is reasonable to consider the likelihood of Alexander and the little Gore girl being included in those photographs.

After a time, Alexander moved on to New Zealand and then South Africa, working all the time. The funds he accumulated enabled him to buy land in the Bethlehem district of Orange Free State and establish a farm, initially living in a tin hut. And then the Boer War started.

During the conflict, Alexander opposed the Commonwealth forces. After peace was agreed, he received his discharge papers from General Botha, who led the Boers and had become famous for capturing Winston Churchill. Incredible as it now seems, Alexander was fighting against his second cousins, Albert and William Thom from Australia, and his second cousin-once-removed, Frederick E. C. Pilkington, who was killed in combat. Further, Alexander's brother Dillon Turner was supporting the British effort in Kimberley.

In 1909, Alexander's father became ill, prompting him to return home in accordance with his father's wishes. During his time at home, he met his future wife, Sarah Paine Murphy. She was the youngest of thirteen children of Sarah and William Murphy J.P., of The Lodge, Kiltegan, County Carlow. They were engaged within two months. Alexander wanted to return alone to South Africa to build a house before Sarah came out to him, but she wouldn't hear of it. They were married in St George's Church in Dublin in June 1910 and had their honeymoon on board ship, bound for Africa. They lived in the tin hut for about a year until a nice little house, which they called Beauparc, was completed. Sarah had always ridden a lot and, in fact, was a very good horse-woman, so they rode a lot together and appeared to have had some great times. She returned to Ireland in 1914 for six months to see her parents, both of whom had suffered strokes and were dying. During this time, she spent a little time at Cullen, finding Mary Ann as difficult as ever, but she could cope with that. Mary Ann offered Cullen to Alexander and Sarah on the condition that Mary Ann could retain two rooms for herself. The offer was conveyed back to South Africa, where Alexander rejected the idea out of hand.

Sarah lost a baby boy around 1916. A daughter, Sarah Watson (id. 7.040), was born two years later at Rietz, Orange Free State, South Africa. By 1920, Mary Ann had decided to live at her son Frederick's home, leaving Cullen to Alexander and Sarah, without any ties. The farm employed eight people at the time.

Alexander and Sarah returned and proceeded to establish a herd of Aberdeen Angus cattle for breeding. The farm in South Africa was passed over to Sarah Watson (Sally) and for some years was let and looked after by a friend of Alexander. It eventually was sold, thus enabling Sally's husband to set up his radiology practice in Dublin and for them to retain Cullen. Sally relates the story of occasional visits to her mother's parents' old family home.

Sadly, it is not really well kept now, but on one occasion, I was taken to a horse stable in the yard to see the names of the whole Murphy family carved in the back of the door.

A circa 1910 portrait of Alexander is shown as Figure 19. He died in 1951, aged eighty-six, and Sarah, known within the family as Daisy, died just over a year later, aged seventy-one. Both are buried in Slane, next to John Bolton. Sally married Herbert John Reid (Shan) Henderson (id. 7.040A) of St Clears, Carmarthen, at St Patrick's Church in Slane, and they lived their whole married life at Cullen. Shan had graduated in medicine from Trinity College in 1938 and radiology in 1945 after war service. His hobby was flying both gliders and powered aircraft. Sally continued breeding Aberdeen Angus cattle and was actively involved in their show judging. The farmland was reduced over the years to sixty acres. Cullen House, shown as Figure 20, and the remaining land were sold after Sally's death in 1999.

Figure 19: Alexander Thom, circa 1910

Figure 20: Cullen House, Slane

Dillon Turner Thom (id. 6.014)

Dillon was the third son of Walter and Mary Ann; he was born in 1868. A treasured lock of his hair, dated 12 September 1872, is held by his granddaughter Rosemary Coffey. Like all his brothers, Dillon was educated in Dublin until his father Walter and family moved to Cullen in 1880. In 1898, Dillon married Mary Evelyn d'Bentley (id. 6.014A) at St Phillip's Church, Milltown. She was the eldest daughter of Henry d'Bentley M.D., of Shannon View, O'Brien's Bridge, County Clare, and Mrs d'Bentley of 45 Palmerston Road, Dublin. Her grandfather was J. W. Seward J.P., of Dromaan House, County Galway. The d'Bentley family tree has been traced back to 1609. The marriage was reported in the 12 November 1898 edition of *Lady's Pictorial*, London (see Figure 21).

Figure 21: Mary Evelyn d'Bentley and Dillon Turner Thom

On 2 December 1898, shortly after their marriage, Dillon and Mary Evelyn (May to everybody in the family) departed from

Southampton on Union Line's SS *Jaul*, heading for Cape Town. Dillon was going to work for DeBeers in the diamond mines at Kimberley. His timing could not have been worse. Not long after his arrival the Boer War started, and the British garrison at Kimberley came under siege by the Afrikaaners for four months, from 11 October 1899 until 15 February 1900. Dillon initially joined the Diamond Field Horse, later transferring to the Kimberley Town Guard, being attached to the Kimberley Buffs, Fifth Division, based at the Belgravia Mine Fort. Three weeks after the siege started, Mary Evelyn gave birth to a son, Henry Bentley (id. 7.025). The plight of the family was widely reported in the English and Irish newspapers, and Henry became known as 'The Siege Baby'. Two years later, as peace was being negotiated, Dillon and family returned to Ireland and re-established themselves at Cullen, assisting the ageing Walter. Dillon and Mary Evelyn produced another three sons: Walter Dillon (id. 7.027), born 1902; Alexander Seward Dillon (id. 7.028), born 1904; and Bolton Dillon (id. 7.031), born 1906.

After his father Walter died in 1909, Dillon moved to a new family home, Kimberley, in Cowper Road, Dublin. He enlisted in the Army on 1 January 1915, soon after World War I was declared. He nominated to join either the Armed Services Corps or the infantry, citing that he was capable of riding. He stated that he had served as a volunteer in the Laingburg Campaign in South Africa in 1894-95, as well as serving in the second Boer War of 1899-1902. The first claim is questionable, given that the first Boer War covered the period 1880-1881. However, it should also be noted that in the newspaper coverage of his wedding, the groom was said to be from Kimberley, South Africa, so it is possible that he lived there for more than half of the 1890s. In the World War I conflict, he served as a munitions inspector in England. In 1926, he lost his eldest son, Henry. Dillon suffered another blow a few years later when Mary Evelyn died in 1934. She is buried at Mt Jerome. He re-married the following year at St Patrick's Church, Dalkey. His second wife, Evelyn (Eva) Constance Russell (id. 6.014B), of Beltroon, Briffni Road, Sandycove, was a cousin of the then-Duke of Bedford. Eva died in 1952, and Dillon died five years later at the ripe old age of eighty-nine. He and his second wife are interred together at 45 E St Nessan at Deansgrange Cemetery, Dublin. The lives of Dillon's four sons are described below:

Henry Bentley Thom (id. 7.025)

The infant known initially as 'The Siege Baby' later acquired the nickname Chip, which remained with him for the rest of his relatively short life. Henry adopted the Christian Scientist religion as an adult. During the postal strike of 1922, he drove a postal van, for which he received the personal thanks of the Minister of Posts and Telegraphs. Henry then became a motor dealer, based in Baggot Street, Dublin. He retired from that business due to illness and died of peritonitis in 1926, aged twenty-six. He is buried in the family vault at Mt. Jerome.

Walter Dillon Thom (id. 7.027)

Walter, the second son, migrated to Argentina in 1923 and settled there for life. His story, and that of his descendants, is told in chapter 8.

Alexander Seward Dillon Thom (id. 7.028)

Alex, the third son, devoted his whole working life, 1920 to 1963, to the Royal Insurance Company, finishing his career as the manager responsible for Dublin. He was based in Kilkenny from 1925 till 1937 but was in the capital for the remainder of the time. Alex survived two wives: Doris, who died in 1953, and Carol, who died in 1974. There were no children from either marriage. Alex had been chairman of the Mt. Jerome Cemetery Trust but was buried at Enniskerry in 1986.

Bolton Dillon Thom (id. 7.031)

Bolton, the youngest son, also was a devoted one-company man. He joined Wallace Bros. in 1923, became a company director just six years later, and was managing director for many years. The company's business interests embraced coal, bricks, and laundry. He and his wife, Wilhelmina, produced four daughters: Margaret, who lives in England; Barbara, who lives in Ireland; and Rosemary and Hilary, both of whom live in Northern Ireland. All daughters married and have continued the bloodline, if not the family name. Bolton and family lived at 47 Arkendale Road, Dublin, during the girls' childhoods. After Wilhelmina died in 1959, aged fifty-three, Bolton moved to 1 Saval Park Gardens, Dalkey, Dublin. He died in 1982, aged seventy-five.

Bolton was a hoarder of all things historic to the family Thom, and an inspiration to me to continue his work. My diary entry on that first visit to Dublin in 1977 says it all. Bolton at the time was also hosting his brother Alex, recovering after hospitalisation.

At 12 midnight, Alex retired; not bad for a seventy-five-year-old out of hospital today. I went to bed at 1 a.m., leaving Bolton to it. I arose at 8.30 a.m. for the planned 9 o'clock breakfast, only to learn that Bolton had retired not just after 1 a.m., but at 3 o'clock. In the intervening period, he had dug out some extremely old and valuable family history documents ready for me to peruse. He also had worked on the family heirloom grandfather clock, which had been a little troublesome of late. He told me he never goes to bed the same day that he woke up.

CHAPTER 8

WALTER DILLON OF ARGENTINA

This chapter relates to Walter Dillon Thom (id. 7.027), the second son of Dillon Turner and Mary Evelyn.

Walter Dillon was born in Dublin in 1902, just after his parents returned from South Africa at the end of the Boer War. He was educated in Dublin. In 1923, he migrated to Argentina and spent most of the rest of his life there. His first job was in the Buenos Aires province breeding race horses, but he could not see much future in that. He moved to a management position on a large farm in the province of Chaco/Santa Fe, where he met his wife-to-be, Daphne King (id. 7.027A). She was the second daughter of the late Mr Thomas E and Mrs King of Las Palmas, Chaco, and formerly of Australia. Their marriage at Las Palmas was reported in the 31 March 1926 edition of the *Irish Times*. Their family tree is shown as Appendix 18.

The King family presence in Argentina is an interesting side story. Daphne's parents were members of a utopian socialist settlement established in Paraguay by a group of Australians in the 1890s. The New Australian Movement, officially called Colonia Nueva Australia, was established near Villarica, 176 km south-east of the capital Asuncion, on 463,000 acres of land granted to it by the government. Its leader was William Lane, a prominent figure in the Australian labour movement, who had become disenchanted and decided to establish a new society outside Australia. The society was based on a common-hold rather than a common-wealth; a brotherhood of English-speaking whites; marriage for life; preservation of the colour line; teetotalism; and communism. His concept of common-hold was that each member of the society should be able to withdraw his proportion of the society's wealth if he chose to leave.

On 16 July 1893, the first group of 238 adults and children departed Sydney on the *Royal Tar*, bought specifically for transporting settlers. They established their new settlement on 28 September 1893, just six days after landing at Asuncion. A second group departed Adelaide three months later, arriving early 1894. By then, problems had arisen in the community because of the prohibition of alcohol, relations with the locals, and Lane's leadership. Lane and fifty-eight others packed their bags and established another colony at Cosme, seventy-two kilometres to the south. Frederick Kidd, who had arrived in the second group from Australia became the new leader. It is understood Daphne's parents were related to Kidd and probably also were members of that second group of settlers.

Crop failures and ongoing instability within the community, together with the loss of an annual government grant conditional on it attracting 1000 members by 1896, resulted in the collapse of the settlement. Some settlers stayed and were given their own piece of land, some moved to Argentina, and some returned home. The Cosme settlement also failed, and William Lane returned to Australia to establish a new life as a respected journalist. He eventually found his way to New Zealand, espousing conservative political beliefs totally opposed to those he held earlier in life.

Daphne's parents moved to Argentina, settling in Las Palmas in the province of Formosa. Daphne's father worked in the local sugar mill. Daphne and her sister Elma were born and grew up there. By the mid-1920s, Walter Thom was running an estancia nearby and was drawn to Las Palmas because of its English-speaking community. It was there he met Daphne. By that time, Daphne's father had died in unusual circumstances—his wife dreamt he was assassinated by locals, and later that day, he suffered that very fate.

Some time after marriage, Walter joined a British cattle firm, Liebig's Extract of Meat Co. Ltd. at the Paso Rodas farm in Corrientes. A series of promotions to larger and more important farms followed, including to Curuzu-Laurel and Santa Julia, eight leagues distant, which he managed. When these properties eventually were sold, he returned to Ireland with the intention of re-establishing himself there, but after seeing the different cattle-breeding techniques employed back home, he soon returned to Argentina. He rejoined Liebig as a cattle buyer in Corrientes. After several years his responsibilities grew, necessitating his relocation to Mercedes. He retired in 1960 after a total of thirty years with Liebig, but continued in the industry selling veterinary products until his death in 1965. Both he and his wife, who predeceased him by almost twenty years, are buried in the British Cemetery in Buenos

Aires. Walter and Daphne are shown in Figures 22 and 23. They raised two children. A middle child had died at birth, unnamed.

Figure 22: Walter Dillon Thom

Figure 23: Daphne King

Henry Edward Dillon Thom (id. 8.013)

Harry was born in 1926 at Puerto Tural, Resistencia, in the province of Chaco, and educated at St George's College in Quilmes, finishing his schooling in 1944. He applied to join the British Navy but was turned down on medical grounds. He joined Liebig as a cadet in Santa Fe Province and progressed over the years as camp manager of increasingly important camps, including one at Entre-Rios. He then moved to Mercedes, working with his father, and succeeded him as cattle buyer for Liebig in 1960. In the meantime, he had married a local girl, Aurora Del Carmen Vargas (id. 8.013A). He retired from Liebig in 1965 and continued working in his own practice. He died in 2003 and is buried at Mercedes.

Daphne Evelyn Patricia Thom (id. 8.020)

Pat was born in 1932 in Corrientes Province and educated in Chaco Province. Her second given name was incorrectly registered at birth as Euclen. She and husband Bob Sword have lived on Estancia Buena Esperanza, a large farm, since their marriage in 1952. The Sword family is listed in Burke's *Landed Gentry*, 18th edition, Volume 3, published 1972. Bob is listed as having served in World War II as a lieutenant in the Royal Navy Volunteer Reserve, after being educated at Charterhouse in England. An early 1990s photograph (see Figure 24) shows some of the Argentinian branch of the family.

Figure 24: (l-r) Bob and Pat Sword, Marie Lou Sword,
Roberto Matarazzo, Rupert and Jane Sword, Harry Thom.

The farm, or estancia in the local Spanish language, was established 130 years ago, and the 'H' branding sign for its stock reflects an earlier ownership by the Hope family. Bob Sword's grandfather purchased the property early last century. Its prime business is breeding cattle and sheep. Over the years, the farm has been reduced in size to its current 5,500 hectares, though in 1993 when I visited, there were still forty-two workers, and 700 workhorses; no motorcycles on this farm!

It is not intended to cover the lives and exploits of the later generations of the Thom family, other than when someone from those generations has reached a level of achievement in life which merits and enjoys respect from the broader community. Rupert Robert Sword (id. 9.017) satisfies that requirement. Like his father, he was educated at Charterhouse before he went on to Nottingham

University. Rupert is Chairman and Regional Head, Latin America, Schroder Investment Management, Schroders plc. In the 2009 New Year's Honours List, he was appointed an Officer, Civil Division, of The Most Excellent Order of the British Empire, for services to British commercial interests and the British community in Argentina. He received this distinction from Queen Elizabeth II at an investiture ceremony held at Buckingham Palace on 10 July 2009. The appointment carries the title OBE.

CHAPTER 9

ROBERT OF AUSTRALIA

This chapter relates to Robert (id. 5.008), the eighth child of Alex and Maria, and the youngest of the three brothers to continue the family line.

Robert was born in Dublin on 6 May 1837. Nothing is known of his childhood days, but it is reasonable to assume that his father Alex, a disciplinarian by nature, would have insisted that all his children had a proper education. It appears the disciplinary streak in Alex did not carry through to either Walter or Robert, both of whom preferred the trappings of a privileged upbringing and an active social life, rather than actually working for a living. Neither of them had any interest in their father's thriving printing business. Doubtless this rather displeased Alex, who could not abide their behaviour. He found a solution for Walter's behaviour by apprenticing him to a local farmer. For whatever reason, he didn't or couldn't find a similar solution for Robert.

It is understood that Robert was more deeply affected than his siblings by the death of his mother and more vocal in his denunciation of the influence over Alex of the woman who would later become his father's second wife. Alex's solution to this dilemma was to offer a £200 annuity to Robert on the condition that he left Ireland and did not return. This conditional annuity was subsequently documented in Alex's 1877 will and later codicils, by which time Robert had been settled in Australia for seven or more years, living well on his father's generous remittance.

It is not known how or when Robert came to Australia. An old handwritten note in my possession states that Robert came to Geelong 1 October 1869. The note was written after Robert's death and lists many of his grandchildren, thus dating it as not earlier than 1927. Immigration records for the period 1855 to 1871 when he married in Geelong, do not show him arriving in Australia. Incomplete and/or inaccurate Australian immigration records have presented a problem to enough researchers as to have prompted the writing of the book *He Must Have Swum*, but we could reasonably dismiss that option for Robert.

Robert settled on the Bellarine Peninsula and lived there until his death in 1892. On 1 March 1871, he married Annie Cox (id. 5.008A) at Christ Church (Church of England), Moorabool Street, Geelong, where she had been baptised on 29 May 1853. She was the first of nine children born to William Cox, a shoemaker from Kenilworth, Warwickshire, and Alice (nee Pywell), who had married on 19 April 1852 at Spondon, Derbyshire. William, born in Kenilworth in February 1830, was the son of John Cox and Ann (nee Parker), who had married on 13 October 1829 at St Nicholas' Church, Kenilworth. Alice, born in 1832, was the first child of

Nathaniel and Catherine Pywell, born 17 May 1809. William and Alice Cox sailed from Liverpool on 16 September 1852 on the *James Brown* and reached Geelong on 5 January 1853. Annie was born a few months later. Around 1856, William Cox moved to Indented Head on the Bellarine Peninsula, twenty-five miles east of Geelong, where he, together with his father-in-law Nathaniel Pywell (who had migrated to Australia on the same ship), leased several acres of land for grazing and cropping. On 5 July 1878, *The Argus* newspaper reported that labourer William Cox had been admitted to Geelong Hospital after attempting suicide by taking strychnine. He appeared before the bench of magistrates the following day and was remanded to Drysdale. On 17 July 1879, the same newspaper reported that Cox, of late a storekeeper, was declared insolvent due to pressure from a principal creditor, and illness of self and family. Interestingly, this insolvency was declared even though his assets totalled £417.1s.8d and his liabilities £303.8s.8d for a surplus of £113.13s; or perhaps it was just bad reporting. In 1897, William and Alice moved to Fremantle, Western Australia, possibly as a result of the drought in Victoria at that time. Alice died there in 1908, as did William the following year, both of senile decay.

Robert's annuity from his father exceeded the wages of two adult men, enabling him generally to avoid work for the rest of his life. He described himself as a gentleman, or sometimes, a farmer. Robert and Annie had seven children over the period 1873 to 1885, all of them born on the Bellarine Peninsula (see Appendix 15). Only three had family. The lives of the seven are described below.

Victoria Maria Annie Dillon Thom (id. 6.019)

Victoria was born in 1873 at Wattle Cottage, the family home. She was registered as a student at Portarlington Common School No. 1251 commencing August 1877, aged four. The writer holds a church hymn book given to Victoria on her thirteenth birthday by her father and inscribed: 'To V.M.A.D. Thom from her affectionate father R.T. 29.1.1886'. It would have been with a heavy heart that only eighteen months later, he added a second inscription: 'Died Geelong August 21, 1887'. The *Geelong Advertiser* of 26 August 1887 reported she had died in Geelong Hospital.

Alice Margaret Kathleen Eva Thom (id. 6.022)

Eva was born in 1874. She was registered as a student at Portarlington State School No. 2455, commencing September 1888 aged thirteen, and leaving in May 1889. Figure 25 is a photograph of her, inscribed: '28.9.91. Seventeen today. To Aunt Maria, from Eva. Wishing you a Merry Xmas and Happy New Year. Eva'. The early posting for Christmas was because of mail delivery times to England. The inscription was in Robert's handwriting, and he had initialled it. The significance of this was not apparent until I sighted Eva's death certificate; clearly Eva was incapable of writing even that simple message. In 1908, aged thirty-four, childless and single, Eva died of pneumonia in Wendouree Mental Asylum near Ballarat. No family detail was included other than her birthplace, suggesting she may have been abandoned by the family some time earlier.

Figure 25: Eva Thom, 1891

Fanny Albert Cora Jane Thom (id. 6.024)

Fanny was born in 1876. She was registered as a student at Portarlington State School, commencing July 1890, aged thirteen. (Presumably there were other earlier registers, since lost, recording Fanny as a student at a much younger age). Fanny married William Henderson (id. 6.024A) in 1896, and their descendants make up a substantial portion of the current Thom family in Australia. Their family tree is shown as Appendix 19. Fanny and William had two children: Holly (id. 7.023), born 1897, and Clarence (id. 7.024), born 1898. Figure 26 shows them in 1905. The family then moved from Geelong to Allambee Reserve in Gippsland, where they farmed and where the children were schooled. A third child Nelson (id. 7.030), died of sunstroke in 1909, aged three. A fourth child Albertha (id. 7.038), known as Bertha, was born in 1916.

Figure 26: Fanny Henderson Family, 1905

After being burnt out by bushfires in 1926, Fanny and William moved to Yarragon. William worked in a sawmill at nearby Thorpdale. An interesting but unfortunate coincidence within Fanny's family is that one of Holly's sons, also named Nelson (id. 8.035), suffered mental retardation with epilepsy and died in Ararat Mental Hospital, aged twenty-five, after twenty-two years of institutionalisation.

Around 1941, Fanny, William, Bertha and her first husband Eric Fowler (id. 7.038A) moved to Brunswick, as there was no work available in Gippsland. The families of both other daughter Holly and son Clarrie also moved to the same suburb. Holly had married Tom Budd (id. 7.023A), who migrated from England in 1912. Clarrie had married Iris Berry (id. 7.024A), whose parents had employed him on their farm at Childers, near Trafalgar. Around 1950, Bertha tried her hand at an East Brunswick mixed business, but in 1953 contracted tuberculosis and spent two years in Greenvale Hospital. Along the way, she had married a second time, to Frank Henderson (id. 7.038B), reportedly a cousin. After her mother died in 1961, Bertha became partner in a farm at Trafalgar with Wattie Chuck (id. 7.038C), whom she later married. Then followed another farm at Mirboo North, but she died shortly thereafter. Clarrie and Iris spent the rest of their lives in Brunswick.

Albert Charles Alexander Robert Thom (id. 6.026)

Albert was born in 1878. He was registered as a student at Portarlington State School, commencing September 1888, aged ten. As young men, Albert and his younger brother William Nathaniel Walter Hamlet (id. 6.028) moved to Bunbury, Western Australia, probably looking for work there. On 18 April 1902, they enlisted in the Australian Commonwealth Horse (WA) for service in South Africa against the Boers. Albert registered as a baker, and William as a groom. They both identified their married elder sister Fanny Henderson of 49 McArthur Place, Carlton, Victoria as next of kin, which suggests they were not close to their mother Annie.

Albert and William were assigned to D Squad of the Eighth Battalion. They departed Australia 2 June 1902. Both were ranked trooper and assigned to No. 4 Troop in the County Districts. They would not have engaged in actual military conflict, as peace was declared on 31 May. They returned to Australia on 24 July. Figure

27 shows them in uniform on return. Albert then went farming at Bannockburn, west of Geelong. He married Elizabeth Gray (id. 6.026A), gentlewoman and the daughter of Robert Gray, gentleman, and wife Mary Ann (nee Mitchell) of Bella Vista, Portarlington at Ryrie St. Presbyterian Church, Geelong, in 1914. The outbreak of World War I prompted Albert to re-enlist in the Australian Army on 24 August 1915. He nominated his wife as next of kin and her address as c/o Bannockburn Post Office, then amended it to Lakes Entrance, and finally to Bella Vista at Portarlington. He allotted two-fifths of his army pay to her. His unit embarked from Melbourne on the HMAT *A68 Anchises* two days later. Lance Corporal Albert Thom, Serial No. 2050 of the Twenty-first Battalion, Third Reinforcement, who had been mentioned in dispatches by General Birdwood, died of wounds on 13 October 1918 in France, less than a month before the armistice. He is buried in Block S, Plot II, Row V, Grave 1 of St Sever Cemetery Extension, near Rouen, France. The headstone is inscribed: 'He died as he lived—a man.' Albert is listed on Panel 95 of the Roll of Honour at the Australian War Memorial in Canberra.

Figure 27: Albert and William Thom, 1902

William Nathaniel Walter Hamlet Thom (id. 6.027)

William was born towards the end of 1880 and died at four months of age. His death is confirmed on his father Robert's death certificate.

William Nathaniel Walter Hamlet Thom (id. 6.028)

The second William was born late in 1881. Given the then-high rate of infant mortality, it was not uncommon after such a death to adopt the same name for the next baby of that sex. William was registered as a student at Portarlington State School, commencing July 1890, aged eight years. As noted above, William (Will) fought in the Boer War with his brother Albert. His discharge certificate, No. 08/485, records that he spent forty-seven days abroad and that he received no medals or decorations. On discharge at Perth, he was twenty years of age, 5 ft 6¼ inches tall, with fair complexion, brown hair, and blue eyes. In 1905, he married Lilian Potter (id. 6.028A), the daughter of Samuel Potter and wife Harriet (nee Getsom). Their wedding photo is shown as Figure 28, and their family tree is shown as Appendix 20. William and Lily had three children: Gladys (id. 7.032), born 1906 at Yarragon, but who died aged three; Geoffrey (id. 7.034), born 1910 at Geelong; and Albert (id. 7.036), born 1911 in Gippsland. In 1909, a Thom still-born baby, almost certainly a sibling, was buried at East Geelong Cemetery. The descendants of Geoffrey (Geoff) and Albert (Bert) represent a modest portion of the current Thom family in Australia.

Figure 28: William Thom and Lily Potter, 1905

Victorian electoral rolls show that William and family lived in the electorates of Corio in 1909, Gippsland in 1914, the Mallee in 1919, and Corio again in 1924. On returning to Geelong, William worked as a labourer at Fyansford Cement Works, as a baker at Potter's Bakery, and then as a boiler attendant at Geelong Hospital until retirement. For some of that time, his address was McDougall Street, Geelong West, but the long-term family home was at 77 West Melbourne Road, Manifold Heights, until Lily's death in 1947. William remarried the following year, only for his second wife Lucy to pass away five years later. He died in 1957. Years later, the old family home site was redeveloped, and it is believed the house itself was relocated three kilometres to 34 Pescott St., Newtown, where it still stands.

Mabel Beatrice Louisa Jane Thom (id. 6.029)

Mabel was born in 1885; she was the last born of the global Generation 6, whose birthdates spanned a period of forty years. Mabel was registered as a student at Portarlington State School, commencing July 1890, aged five. In 1903, being only eighteen years of age, she had to seek her mother's consent to marry James Hind (id. 6.029A). The descendants of Mabel and James make up a substantial portion of the current Thom family in Australia, and their family tree is shown as Appendix 21. At one time, Mabel lived at 159 Fyans Street, Marnock Vale, in the Geelong area. Figure 29 shows Mabel later in life.

Figure 29: Mabel Hind

The *Geelong Advertiser* mentioned Robert Thom and his family on several occasions over the years till his death in 1892.

May 7, 1874: Robert was appointed correspondent of payment, Board of Advice, No. 96.

February 21, 1876: That pleasant and picturesque little spot along the shores of Port Phillip Bay, Portarlington, seems to have been greatly disturbed by the eccentricities of Thomas Thom. This unfortunate fellow furnishes additional evidence, if that were needed, of what might become of a man in Victoria. Thom is the son of the renowned printer and publisher of 87 and 88 Abbey Street, Dublin, and is in regular receipt of money from his indulgent parent. Like many others similarly situated, Thomas Thom is addicted to the excessive use of intoxicating liquors, and whilst leading an unostentatious kind of existence in a pretty seaside township, is quite indifferent as to the sources from which he obtains supplies. The degrading habit of drinking has thus brought low one who at an earlier period of his life promised something better than the ignominious career of a drunkard and a disturber of the peace.

A précis of the above *Geelong Advertiser* extract, compiled by the Geelong Historical Centre, adds that in court three days earlier, Thom was bound over on two sureties of £10 to keep the peace for six months; he had threatened his wife and a neighbour. The reference to Robert as Thomas was a reporting error by the newspaper.

June 27, 1876: Robert resigned from the Board of Advice.

April 23, 1877: Notice was given of the auction of Robert Thom's Wattle Cottage and twenty acres of choice onion land at Portarlington on 2 May 1877.

May 28, 1878: Mrs Robert Thom gave birth to Albert at Wattle Cottage. (This suggests the property either did not sell at auction or was now leased back.)

November 25, 1897: William Higgins was appointed executor of Robert Thom's estate.

Robert divorced Annie in 1890. The Public Records File No.1885/90-853 is not accessible to the public. *The Argus* newspaper of 20 December 1890 reported:

Friday December 19, 1890, before Mr Justice Webb. Robert Thom petitioned for dissolution of his marriage with Annie Thom, formerly

Cox, on the ground of desertion, and also of adultery with William Baker, a groom. The parties were married in 1871, and in 1881 the respondent went away with the co-respondent, with whom she subsequently lived. His Honour granted a decree nisi, with costs. Mr Forlonge appeared for the petitioner. The case was undefended.

It is likely that the separation of Robert and Annie was a little more complicated than as reported above. In 1881, Annie lost an infant son and gave birth to another, and in 1885 she gave birth to a daughter. Robert is recorded as being the father of all three progeny. As a consequence of the divorce, Annie lost all subsequent rights to the £100 annuity specified in the will of Robert's father, conditional on her remaining Robert's widow and remaining out of Ireland. It is not known with which of the parents the children of the marriage lived subsequent to the divorce. A photograph of Robert taken in 1890 by electric light is shown as Figure 30.

Figure 30: Robert Thom, 1890

Robert died intestate on 25 July 1892 of acute meningitis and heart failure after eight days of illness. His death certificate records his address as St Leonards, a small village near Portarlington, where he was buried. It also records his mother as Lady Dillon, her preferred name. The informant to the death certificate, Edwin Seivers, described as a friend but in fact also a relative by marriage, advised that Robert had lived in Victoria for thirty-two years, i.e., since 1860. That statement is believed to be in error by about ten years, as there is no evidence supporting that earlier migration. The probate jurisdiction of the Supreme Court of Victoria was advised by William Higgins, who was both an administrator of the estate and a creditor. Robert owned no real estate, and his personal estate was limited to household furniture and effects of sworn value not exceeding £10. File No. 66/350 granted 24 December 1897 recorded that no duty was payable on the within letter of administration. Higgins was charged with the responsibility of distributing the estate in accordance with the law.

When Robert's stepmother Sarah died in 1903, she bequeathed £5000 to be shared equally by Robert's surviving children, who by then had effectively reduced to four: Fanny, Albert, William and Mabel. Given that Robert died virtually penniless, Sarah's bequest perhaps explains how William could afford to go farming in Gippsland around 1910 and for Albert to go farming in Bannockburn not long after. It is not known if Annie re-married after her divorce from Robert, or when and where she died. In 1903 whilst living in Brunswick, she gave approval for her under-age daughter Mabel, to marry. It is possible Annie later moved to Western Australia to be with her parents. The 10 June 1909 death certificate of her father records that Annie survived him.

By any measure, Geoffrey Walter Thom (id. 7.034), the elder son of William and Lily, qualifies for specific mention here, based on his achievements in life and his contribution to society. Geoff returned from active service in Papua New Guinea during World War II to establish his own accounting firm. He became a Geelong West councillor in 1946 and progressed to wearing the mayoral robes from 1955 to 1957. During this period, he immersed himself in many community activities and held public offices associated with Geelong's Tourist Authority, Hospital, Marina, University, and Chamber of Commerce, to name but a few. The following year, he won for the centre-right Liberals the South Western Province seat in Victoria's Legislative Council, representing not only Geelong, but also much of the state to the west. He was the government whip from 1964 till 1967 and retired from politics in 1970 due to ill health. He died in 1973. His contribution to the community was recognised in 1987, when a room in the Geelong West Town Hall was named in his honour. In 2009, on completion of the Geelong Bypass leading from Melbourne to the Great Ocean Road, his planning and promotion of that route many years ago were recognised when the two bridges spanning the Barwon River were named after him. The bridges are shown in Figure 31.

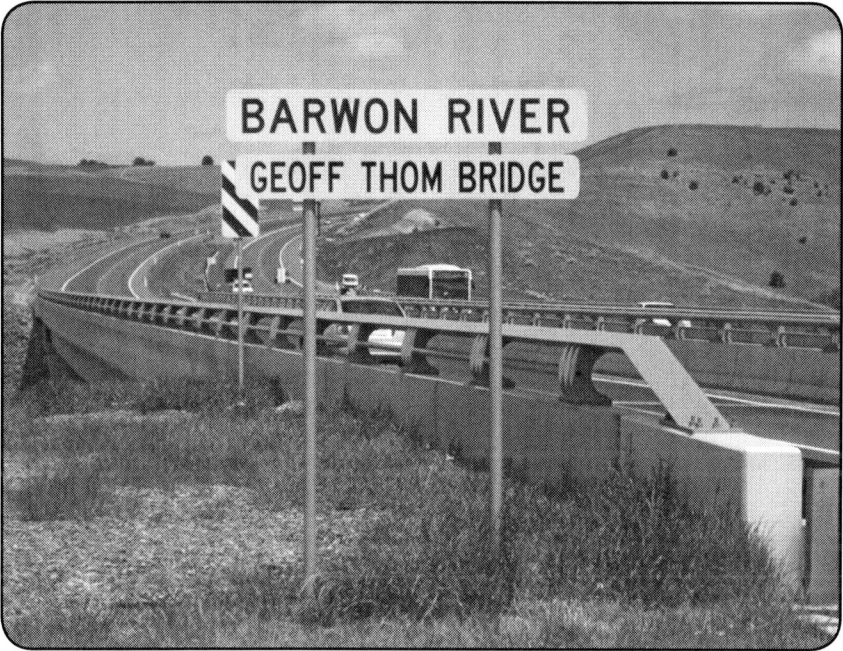

Figure 31: Geoff Thom Bridge

CHAPTER 10

THE FAMILY NAME

In *The Surnames of Scotland, Their Origins, Meaning and History*, by George Francis Black, Ph.D. (1866-1948), the entry for the Thom family name reads:

Thom. A diminutive of Thomas, q.v. Alexander Thome appears as vicar of Stracathro in 1433 and 1447 . . . Jok Tom was tenant in Balgreschac, 1473 . . . Andree Thome held a tenement in Glasgow before 1487, and reference is made in 1497 to the tenement of quondam Walter Thome there . . . A fourth part of the vill of Westirparsy was leased to Alexander Thome and his son Alexandeer Thome in 1485 . . . William Thom was witness in Dundrennan in 1545 . . . Alexander Thome had a tack of a fourth part of Cotzardis in 1555, and Johne Thome a tack of an eighth part of the lands of Wester Balbrogy at the same time . . . James Thome to stand in sackcloth for quarrelling in time of divine service, 1681 . . . Patrick Thome was merchant burgess of Edinburgh, 1673 . . . In 1561 we have an instance of Thom as a forename in Thom Arnot, member of council of Stirling . . . The founder of the Dublin printing house of Alexander Thom and Co. was a native of Aberdeen. Thom is also used as an anglicised form of MacThom, q.v.Tom 1685.

The last use of the Thome spelling was for a christening in 1745. Mormon records show the Thom family name as early as 1671 in Kincardineshire, but Walter Thom's *The History of Aberdeen* mentions a Bessie Thom being burnt at the stake for witchcraft in 1596. From our earliest-known ancestor, the only known Generation 9 male descendants bearing the family name are Alexander Edward Dillon of Argentina and Fraser Colin McGregor of Australia, son of the writer, so the family name still might carry into the tenth generation. It is not by pure chance that the nominal date of publication of this book coincides with Fraser's wedding day.

The family name in Australia is unique in that the 'th' is sounded as in thistle, versus the alternative pronunciation used in the rest of the world, with a silent 'h', as in Thomas. It was probably during his journey from Ireland to Australia, when there was nobody around who knew any better, or cared, that Robert Thom chose this new pronunciation to further differentiate himself from the family he had left, never to see again.

The family motto 'Dum Vivo Spero' literally means 'Whilst I live, I hope.'

The family crest is described as 'A Dexter Hand Holding a Sword Proper', as noted in Fairbairn's *Book of Crests of the Families of Great Britain and Ireland*. Several pieces of silverware held by the Irish branch of the family incorporate the family crest and the motto, as shown in Figure 32.

Figure 32: Family Crest

The family coat of arms as described in John Burke's *A General Armory of England Scotland and Ireland* (1842) incorporates a yellow background with a red and white check sash extending from top left to bottom right. A modern interpretation of this coat of arms is shown in Figure 33.

Figure 33: Coat of Arms

Statistics and factual data on the global family are included in Appendix 22.

APPENDIX 1

MAP OF NORTH EAST SCOTLAND

© Nicolson Maps
This map has been printed with the permission of Nicolson Maps
Unauthorised reproduction by any means is an infringement of copyright law.
The representation of a road, track or footpath does not guarantee a public right of way.

APPENDIX 2

STATISTICAL ACCOUNT OF SCOTLAND

THE

STATISTICAL ACCOUNT

OF

SCOTLAND.

PARISH OF INVERBERVIE OR BERVIE.

(County of Kincardine, Synod of Angus and Mearns, Presbytery of Fordoun.)

By Mr Walter Thom of Bervie.

Name, Extent, Burgh of Bervie, &c.

THE name seems to be taken from the rivulet of Bervie; with the addition of the Gaelic word *Inver*, which, in its signification, applies particularly to the situation of the town of Inverbervie, but in common writing and speaking is now in disuse. This parish was formerly a part of that of Kinneff; but as there was no bridge on Bervie water, the minister of Kinneff agreed to keep a suffragan

suffragan at Bervie, to accommodate the people in that quarter of his parish; and the Lords for the Plantation of Kirks, in the year 1618, disjoined Bervie from Kinneff, and increased the stipends of both incumbents. The power of presentation is vested in the Crown. The extent of this parish is inconsiderable, being only about 2 miles long, and 1¼ mile broad; from E. to W. it rises in a gradual ascent, and terminates at the top of a high hill. On the east corner of the parish, the burgh of Bervie is situated; and on the southmost part, the village of Gourdon stands. The burgh of Bervie consists of three streets, which form nearly three sides of a square, and contains about 110 dwelling-houses. The original plan of the town seems to have been laid out in a very judicious manner, but it has not been adhered to; for the houses are let down irregularly, according to the fancy of the builders. Bervie is the only royal burgh in the county of the Mearns, and its charter was granted by David II. in the year 1341. When returning from England, he was forced, by stress of weather, to land at the water-mouth of Bervie; and it is said, that having met with great hospitality and kindness from the inhabitants, he bestowed on the town a royalty, as a mark of his particular favour: The place on which he landed, to this day bears his name, and is called Craig David. James VI. in the year 1595, renewed the charter, and confirmed all the privileges and immunities granted by King David*.

Fisheries,

* By this charter, the public property is difficult to be reached out; intended to comprehend nearly the whole extent of the parish, but the property which now belongs to the town is confined to a piece of barren muir, a few acres of rough ground, and a range of braes about a mile or extent, which afford a little grass for the cows belonging to the inhabitants of the burgh, in the summer season. By this charter, "full power is given

APPENDIX 3

THE HISTORY OF ABERDEEN

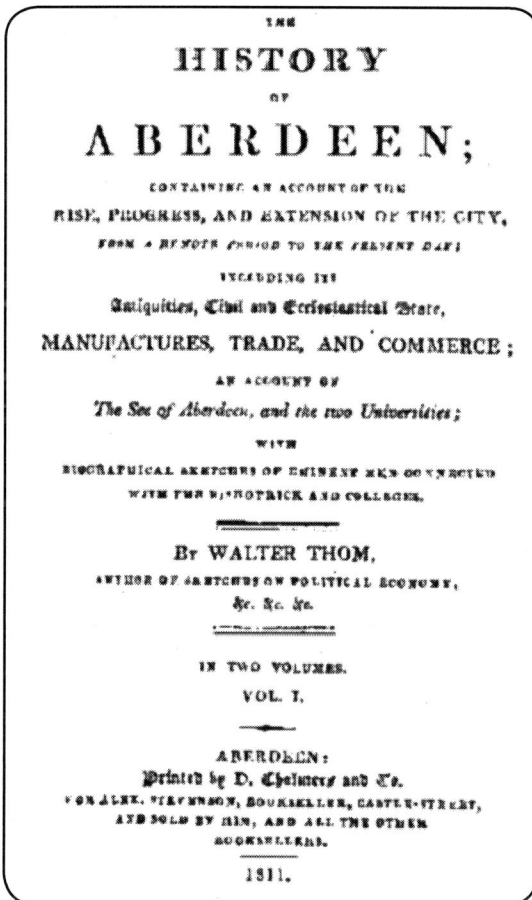

THE

HISTORY

OF

ABERDEEN;

CONTAINING AN ACCOUNT OF THE

RISE, PROGRESS, AND EXTENSION OF THE CITY,

FROM A REMOTE PERIOD TO THE PRESENT DAY;

INCLUDING ITS

Antiquities, Civil and Ecclesiastical State,

MANUFACTURES, TRADE, AND COMMERCE;

AN ACCOUNT OF

The See of Aberdeen, and the two Universities;

WITH

BIOGRAPHICAL SKETCHES OF EMINENT MEN CONNECTED
WITH THE BISHOPRICK AND COLLEGES.

By WALTER THOM,

AUTHOR OF SKETCHES ON POLITICAL ECONOMY,
&c. &c. &c.

IN TWO VOLUMES.

VOL. I.

ABERDEEN:
Printed by D. Chalmers and Co.
FOR ALEX. STEVENSON, BOOKSELLER, CASTLE-STREET,
AND SOLD BY HIM, AND ALL THE OTHER
BOOKSELLERS.

1811.

APPENDIX 4

PEDESTRIANISM

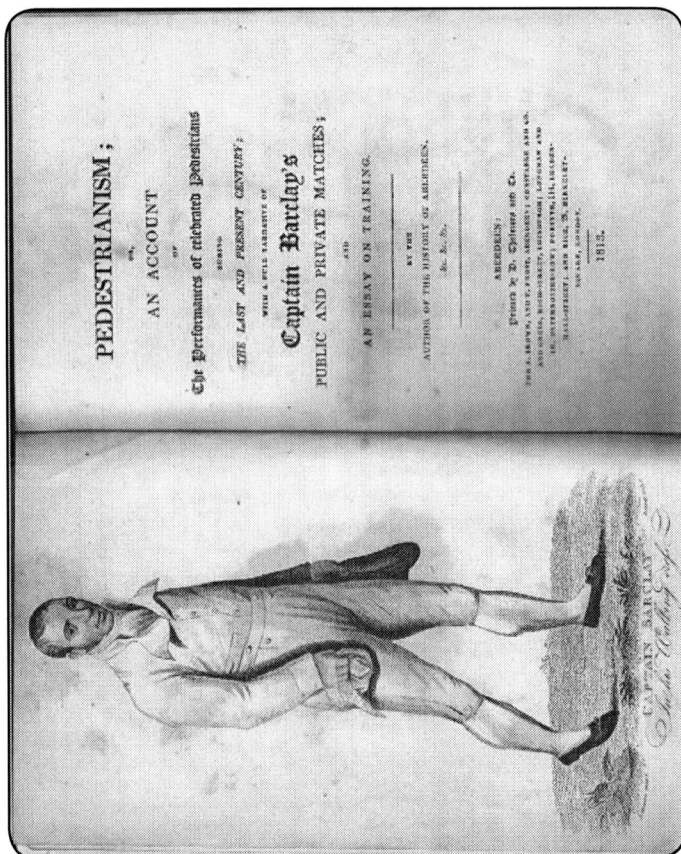

APPENDIX 5

SCIENCE OF POLITICAL ECONOMY

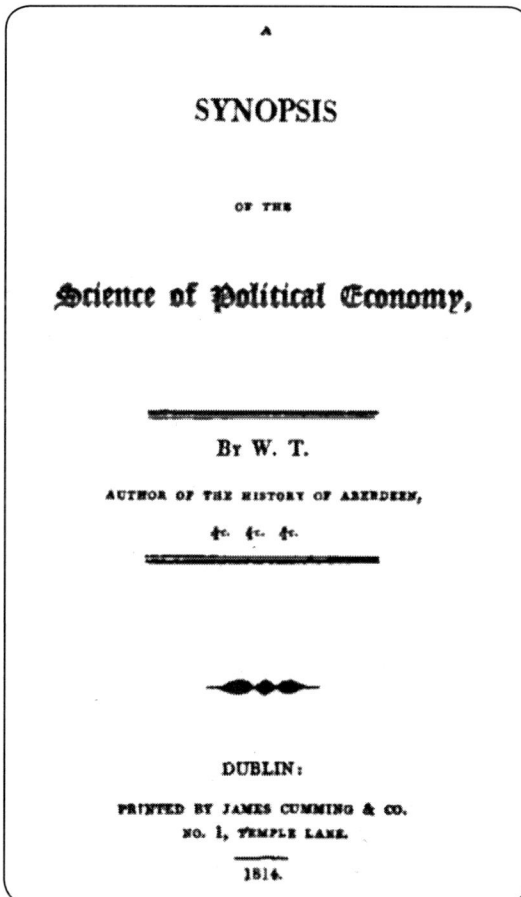

A

SYNOPSIS

OF THE

Science of Political Economy,

By W. T.

AUTHOR OF THE HISTORY OF ABERDEEN,

&c. &c. &c.

DUBLIN:

PRINTED BY JAMES CUMMING & CO.
NO. 1, TEMPLE LANE.

1814.

APPENDIX 6

PRINTING TRADE INDENTURE

This Indenture witnesseth that Patrick Allard of Wellington Street, Dublin, of his own free will and accord and with the consent of his father, doth put himself apprentice to Alexander Thom of 87 Middle Abbey Street, printer to Her Majesty's Public Departments in Ireland, to learn his art as compositor and with him (after the manner of an apprentice) to serve from the first day of July 1863 until the full end and seven years from thence next following, fully to be completed and ended. During this term, the said apprentice his said master faithfully shall serve, his secrets keep, his lawful commands everywhere gladly do. He shall do no damage to his said master nor see it to be done of others, but that he, to the best of his power, shall let or forthwith give warning to his said master of the same. He shall not waste the goods of the said master nor give or lend them unlawfully to any. He shall not contract matrimony within the said term. Hurt to his said master he shall not do or cause or procure to be done by others. He shall not play at cards, dice, tables, or any other unlawful games whereby his said master may have loss with his own or others goods during said term.

Without licence of his said master, he shall neither buy nor sell. He shall not haunt or use taverns, alehouses, or playhouses nor absent himself from his said master's service by day unlawfully; but in all things as an honest and faithful apprentice, he shall behave himself towards his said master and all during the said term. And the said master said apprentice, in the same art which he useth by the best way and means that he can, shall teach and instruct or cause to be taught and instructed, with due correction, finding unto the said apprentice, in lieu of board, etc. for the first year, three shillings per week; for the second year, four shillings per week; for the third year, five shillings per week; for the fourth year, six shillings per week; for the fifth year, seven shillings per week; for the sixth year, eight shillings per week; and for the seventh and last year, ten shillings per week, during the said term. And for the due performance of all and every one of the said covenants and agreements, either of the said parties bindeth himself to the other by these present. In *witness* whereof the parties above named to these *indentures* have interchangeably put their hands and seals, the first day of July, in the year of our Lord, one thousand eight hundred and sixty three (1863).

Signed, sealed, and delivered in the presence of J. D. Scott.

Alec Thom   Seal
Patrick Allard   Seal

APPENDIX 7

APPOINTMENT OF ALEXANDER THOM AS A JUSTICE OF THE PEACE

Victoria by the Grace of God of the United Kingdom of Great Britain and Ireland Queen Defender of the faith and so forth, To Our Trusty and well-beloved Sir Edward Borough, Bart . . . . (plus another 73 persons all listed) . . . . and Alexander Thom Esquire of 87 and 88 Middle Abbey Street and Donnycarney House, Donnycarney. Greeting, whereas, under and by virtue of an Act passed in the Third and Fourth years of Our Reign Chapter One hundred and eight, entitled "An Act for the regulation of Municipal Corporations in Ireland". We reposing special trust and confidence in your fidelity prudence and care Have appointed and by these presents Do appoint you and each of you the said Sir E Borough . . . (plus another 73 persons all listed) . . . . and Alexander Thom, Our Justices to keep the peace within our Borough of Dublin and to keep and cause to be kept all Ordinances and Statutes made for the good of Our Peace, and for the conservation of the same, and for the quiet rule and government of Our people in all and every the Articles thereof within Our Borough aforesaid, according to the force, form and effect thereof: and to chastise and punish all persons offending against the forms of those Ordinances and Statutes or any of them in the Borough aforesaid as according to the form of those Ordinances and Statutes shall be fit to be done; and to cause to come before you or any one or more of you all those persons who shall threaten any of Our people in their persons or with burning their houses, to find sufficient security for the Peace or for their good behaviour towards us and our people: and if they shall refuse to find such security then to cause them to be safely kept in Our prisons until they have found such security. We have also assigned and by these presents do assign you and each of you the said Sir E Borough . . . (plus another 73 persons all listed) . . . . and Alexander Thom Our Justices, to enquire by the Oaths of good and lawful men of the Borough aforesaid, and by all other ways and means by which the truth of the matter may be best known of all and all manner of Treasons, Murders, Manslaughters Burnings Unlawful Assemblies, Felonies, Robberies, Witchcrafts, Enchantments, Sorceries, Magic Arts, Trespasses, Forestallings, Regratings, Engrossings, and Extortions whatsoever, and of all and singular other Misdeeds and Offences of which the Justice of Our Peace can or ought lawfully to enquire by whomsoever and howsoever done or committed, or that hereafter shall there happen howsoever to be done or attempted in the Borough aforesaid, and also of all those who presume by Unlawful Assemblies to be disturbers of Our Peace and of Our people, within the Borough aforesaid: and also of all those who in the Borough aforesaid have either gone or ridden, or that hereafter shall presume to go or ride in Companies with armed force against Our peace, to the disturbance of Our Peace: and also of all those who in like manner have lain in wait, or hereafter shall presume to lie in wait to maim

or kill our people: and also Innholders and of all and singular
other persons who have offended or attempted or hereafter shall
presume to offend or attempt in the abuse of weights or measures
or in the sale of victuals against the forms of the Ordinances and
Statutes or any of them, in that behalf made for the Common good
of Ireland and of our people thereof in the Borough aforesaid;
as also of all Sheriffs, Bailiffs, Seneschals, Constables and other
Officers whomsoever who in the execution of their Offices about
the premises or any of them have unlawfully demeaned themselves
or that hereafter shall presume unlawfully to demean themselves,
or have been or hereafter shall be careless remiss or negligent
in the Borough aforesaid: and of all and singular Articles and
Circumstances and all other things whatsoever by whomsoever
done committed or perpetrated in the Borough aforesaid or that
shall hereafter there happen howsoever to be done or attempted
in anywise more fully concerning the truth of the promises, or
any of them; and to inspect all Indictments whatsoever so before
you taken or to be taken or made before others late Justices of the
Peace in the Borough and not as yet determined and to make or
continue the Process thereupon against all and singular persons
so indicted, or which hereafter shall happen to be indicted before
you until they be apprehended, render themselves or be outlawed
and to hear and determine all and singular the matters aforesaid
(Treason Excepted), according to the Laws and Statutes of Ireland
as in the like case hath been used to be done, and to chastise
and punish the said persons offending, and every of them for
their offences, by fines, ransoms, amerciaments, forfeitures or
otherwise as ought and hath been used to be done according to
the laws and customs of Ireland or the form of the Ordinances
or Statutes aforesaid: and to discharge our Gaols of all Prisoners

therein detained and imprisoned for felonies: Provided always that if a case of difficulty on the Determination of any of the premises shall happen to arise before you or anyone or more of you then do not you or anyone or more of you proceed to give Judgment thereon except it be in the presence of one of Our Justices of one or other Bench or of one of the Barons of our Exchequer or of one of Our Counsel learned in the Laws. And We therefore command you that you and each of you diligently attend the keeping of the Peace, Ordinances and Statutes, and all and singular other the premises, and at certain days and places which you, or any one or more of you, shall in that behalf appoint you or any one or more make enquiry upon the premises (except as before excepted) and perform and fulfil the same in form aforesaid doing therein that which to Justice appertaineth according to the Laws and Customs of Ireland. Saving to us all amerciaments and other things thereof to us belonging, We also command, by virtue of these presents our Sheriff of the Borough aforesaid, that at certain days and places which you, or any one or more of you shall make known unto him, he cause to come before you, or any one or more of you such and so many good and lawful men of his Bailiwick by whom the truth of the matter in the premises may be better known and enquired of. Witness Our Lieutenant General and General Governor of Ireland at Dublin the Eighteenth day of February in the Thirtythird year of our Reign.

APPENDIX 8

APPOINTMENT OF ALEXANDER THOM AS QUEEN'S PRINTER IN IRELAND

Victoria by the Grace of God of the United Kingdom of Great Britain and Ireland Queen defender of the faith and so forth. To all unto whom these presents shall come Greeting.

Whereas it is deemed advisable in order to ensure accuracy in printing Proclamations and Orders in Council that our Trusty and well beloved Alexander Thom Esquire should be appointed our Printer in that part of the United Kingdom of Great Britain and Ireland called Ireland for the above purpose

Know ye therefore that we of our Special Grace certain Knowledge and mere motion by and with the Advice and Consent of out Right Trusty and Knight Entirely beloved Cousin and Councillor James Duke of Abercorn KG our Lieutenant General and General Governor of that part of our United Kingdom called Ireland and according to the tenor and effect of our Letter under our Privy Signet and Royal Sign Manual bearing date at Our Court at Saint Nimess the nineteenth day of February One Thousand Eight Hundred and Seventy Six in the Thirty ninth year of our Reign and now Enrolled in the Record and Writ Office of our High Court of Chancery in that part of our said United Kingdom called Ireland have given and granted and by these presents We do Give and Grant to our Trusty and well beloved Alexander Thom the Office of Our Printer General within that part of our said United Kingdom of Great Britain and Ireland called Ireland.

And we do hereby Give and Grant unto the said Alexander Thom full power and authority for the imprinting distribution and sale within that part of our said United Kingdom called Ireland at such prices as shall be approved by the Controller of the Stationery Office subject however to the condition that such prices shall not be in excess of those charged by our Printers in that part of our said United Kingdom called England of all proclamations and Orders in Council from and after the first day of January last provided his aforesaid authority be confined to the above employment and the printing of the Dublin Gazette.

Provided also that upon the determination at any time of the said authority to the said Alexander Thom he shall not be entitled to any compensation by reason thereof and him the said Alexander Thom our sole Printer General in Ireland. We do by these Presents constitute make ordain and appoint To have hold Exercise and enjoy the said Office with all powers and authorities profits commodities advantages and privileges thereunto belonging or in any wise appertaining unto the said Alexander Thom from and after the said first day of January last during our pleasure.

And We do hereby will and expressly forbid and prohibit all and every Our Subject and all persons whatsoever besides the said Alexander Thom except as hereinbefore is reserved from and after the date of these our Letters Patent during the time hereby granted that they or any of them by themselves or by any others whatsoever do Imprint or cause to be Imprinted within that part of our said United Kingdom called Ireland any of the said Proclamations Orders in Council and the Dublin Gazette or any other printing as shall be published as aforesaid without the Licence of the said Alexander Thom shall be first had and obtained.

And we do hereby of our like special Grace certain knowledge and mere motion by and with the advice and consent aforesaid grant unto the said Alexander Thom during the time hereby granted full power and authority from time to time that he may within that part of our said United Kingdom called Ireland as often as occasion shall require take up such and so many skilful workmen in the Trade Art or Mystery of Printing as he in his discretion shall think fit to work in the said Trade Art or Mystery for such reasonable wages as he the said Alexander Thom shall appoint and for so long a time as he shall want the said Workmen.

And We do strictly charge and consent all and singular Mayors Sheriffs Constables and all other Our Officers and Ministers and loving subjects that they and every one of them be aiding and assisting to the said Alexander Thom in the execution of the said Office and all other matters and things whatsoever herein contained.

Provided always that upon the determination at any time of these our Letters Patent he the said Alexander Thom shall not be entitled to any compensation by reason thereof.

Provided also that this our Grant or anything herein contained shall not in any wise be repugnant or contrary to any Grant already made by us or any like Grant to be made by us our Heirs or Successors to any of our Printers within that part of our said United Kingdom called England or to any of their Deputies or Assigns or any of them

Provided always that these our Letters Patent be Enrolled in the Record and Writ Office of our High Court of Chancery in Ireland aforesaid within the space of six months next ensuing the date of these presents.

In Witness whereof we have caused these our Letters to be made Patent Witness James Duke of Abercorn KG Our Lieutenant General and Governor General of Ireland at Dublin the Sixteenth day of March in the Thirty Ninth year of Our Reign.

APPENDIX 9

OBITUARY ALEX THOM

Obituary Notice

OF THE LATE

ALEXANDER THOM, ESQ, J.P.

QUEEN'S PRINTER IN IRELAND;

A Vice-President

OF THE STATISTICAL AND SOCIAL INQUIRY SOCIETY OF IRELAND.

Prepared by request of the Council, and read at a meeting of the Society on Wednesday, 27th January, 1880.

OBITUARY NOTICE,

ETC.

AT a meeting of the Statistical and Social Inquiry Society of Ireland, held at Leinster Hall, Molesworth-street, Dublin, on Tuesday, 27th January, 1880, PROFESSOR INGRAM, LL.D. F.T.C.D., President, in the chair, Dr. HANCOCK, Hon. Secretary, said:

Since the last meeting of this Society, we have lost one of its original members, Mr. Alexander Thom, who did more to popularize statistics in Ireland and place before the world the real condition of the country than any other member. The Council have requested me to bring under your notice a brief sketch of his life, with special reference to the services he has rendered to Ireland in the matter of statistics.

Mr. Thom was born in Scotland of a good Scotch family, and was educated at the High School of Edinburgh. His maternal grandfather was an esteemed gentleman, Mr. John Turner, of Turner Hall, in Aberdeenshire; his paternal grandfather was a linen manufacturer, and the first to introduce into Scotland a machine for spinning linen yarn. His father, Mr. Walter Thom, was a statistical writer of considerable repute, as appears from the notice of him in *Cates' Dictionary of General Biography.* He wrote an account of his native parish of Barvie, in Aberdeenshire, for Sir John Sinclair's *Statistical Survey of Scotland;* he contributed several articles to Brewster's *Encyclopedia,* and published in 1811 a History of Aberdeen, in which he describes himself as author of *Sketches in Political Economy.*

When the great Sir Robert Peel came over to Ireland as Chief-Secretary, he selected Mr. Walter Thom as editor of the *Dublin*

5

ing for Royal Commissions in Ireland had all been executed in London, but Mr. Drummond was anxious to avoid the delay of that mode of proceeding, and Mr. Thom offered for and obtained the contract, and secured the printing of future Royal Commissions for Dublin.

The great achievement of Mr. Thom's life was his starting, in 1844, his *Irish Almanac and Official Directory*, containing the novel feature of statistics of Ireland.

Whilst he had owed his first start in life to the patronage of Sir Robert Peel, having now arrived at the prime of life, forty-two years of age, he seeks the support of the public on higher and safer ground, indicated in the preface of his first volume, compiled in 1843, for the year 1844, which commences in these terms :—

"In offering a New Almanac and Directory to the notice of the public, the publisher is fully sensible that its title to the patronage he hopes for must rest wholly on its intrinsic merits."

He was spared to the ripe age of seventy-eight to carry out this sound principle of seeking public patronage, and it was only within three months of his death that he transferred his successful printing business to his son-in-law, Mr. Pilkington, to whom he had two years previously transferred his *Almanac*.

As we have seen him prosperous and successful in business, and commanding respect for his intelligence and ability, it is well to bear in mind as some guide for younger men commencing their career, the manly and honest principle he here laid down and ever followed, of endeavouring to deserve public approval by the intrinsic merit of his work.

That first preface of his contains a singular commentary on Irish affairs; it was written in the closing months of 1843, just when the Clontarf meeting had been proclaimed, and information had been filed against O'Connell, Sir John Gray, and others. While statesmen and public writers at a distance thought Ireland so difficult to govern, this naturalised Scotchman, addressing himself with earnestness and

4

Journal, which after the fashion of that day he retained to defend his policy. On Sir Robert Peel retiring from the Chief-Secretaryship in 1817, he handed over the *Dublin Journal* to Mr. Walter Thom, and he appears as proprietor from thenceforward. The prospects of the paper were seriously affected by the changes of imperial policy towards Ireland, introduced by the Marquis of Wellesley when he came over as Lord Lieutenant, in December, 1821. The change was marked by the appointment of Mr., afterwards Lord Plunket, the Protestant champion of Roman Catholic Emancipation, as Attorney-General, in place of Mr. Saurin, who held opposite views.

The *Evening Mail* was started by the Irish opponents of Emancipation, to resist Lord Wellesley's policy, and its extreme views being then more acceptable to Irish Protestants, the *Dublin Journal* consequently became an unsuccessful speculation.

To help his father in this crisis, Mr. Alexander Thom, a young man of twenty, gave up his own prospects in life and devoted his whole energy to keep the paper going as long as his father lived. In the discharge of this filial duty he thoroughly learned the business of printing, and the more important moral lesson of how to struggle against difficulties. His father died in June, 1834, and is buried in St. Luke's church, where there is a monument to his memory. On his death the *Dublin Journal* ceased to exist, and Mr. Alexander Thom sought from Sir Robert Peel some recognition of his father's and his own services. These were rewarded by a contract for printing for the Post Office, and Mr. Thom found a partner to supply the requisite capital to enable him to take advantage of his contract.

The next great step in Mr. Thom's career was his energy in executing the printing for the Irish Railway Commission of 1838, presided over by the celebrated Thomas Drummond, the distinguished Scotchman, who was Under-Secretary for Ireland during the early years of Lord Melbourne's government. Up to that time the print-

intelligence to supply a want in Irish affairs, and to diffuse true and accurate information, found everyone, irrespective of creed or party, ready to assist.

"To those persons to whom the publisher is indebted for aiding in this revision, he feels that his most grateful thanks are due, as well for the cordial alacrity with which they have responded to his applications, and the opinions expressed by them of the manner in which the portions submitted to their inspection have been executed, has been to him a gratifying testimony of the utility of the undertaking."

The early and cordial appreciation which Mr. Thom received helped him in his work, for he adds :—

"Thus encouraged by the favourable opinions of those highly qualified to appreciate the merits of the work, the publisher looks forward to its annual continuance, not merely in its present form, but with such additions and improvements as will render every successive year's publication more worthy of general patronage."

If the compilation which Mr. Thom then commenced, and annually improved for so many years, is creditable to him, the thorough appreciation of it which encouraged him and enabled him to continue it so long, and leave it an institution in the country, is creditable to the Irish public.

The modest term of publisher which Mr. Thom adopted in his prefaces, concealed for many years from all but his intimate friends, the fact that he was author of the compilation himself, and that the whole conception, plan, and continuous improvements were his. This, fortunately, became known in time for this Society to acknowledge his services, by making him first a Vice-President and afterwards offering to him the Presidency of the Society. Though from the pressure of his engagements he declined the preparation of an address and declined the honour, he cordially appreciated the recognition of his work, and he presented the society with £100, which was employed in procuring a valuable series of reports on Irish affairs by Mr. William Graham Brooke, Mr. Mulholland, Mr. Molloy, and Professor Donnell.

When the Peel scholarships in the Queen's Colleges were founded by the present Sir Robert Peel, during his Chief-Secretaryship, in remembrance of the patronage of his father already referred to, Mr. Thom was one of the earliest and most substantial contributors to the fund.

The breadth of view Mr. Thom had of Irish affairs was probably best indicated by his valuable contribution towards the materials of Irish history, in the republication, entirely for gratuitous distribution, of a collection in two volumes, entitled: *Tracts and Treatises Illustrative of the Natural History, Antiquities, and Political and Social State of Ireland at various periods prior to the Present Century*. In these volumes he brought out the works of Boate, Ware, Spenser, and Sir John Davis; also those of Sir William Petty, Bishop Berkeley, Price, and Dobbs. This work of his is so appreciated, that when the volumes he presented turn up at sales of private libraries, they bring two guineas.

We are thus indebted to the munificence of an individual for what in other counties is the work of great societies or of the state. As he has thus preserved the memory of those Irish statisticians and public writers of past centuries, historians in future years, when treating of Irish affairs in the present century, will add the name of Alexander Thom to the honoured list of trustworthy and able writers on Irish affairs.

THE PRESIDENT (John K. Ingram, LL.D.), said—This is not an occasion on which it would be proper to take any formal vote of the Society. But the cordial acclamations with which you have received Dr. Hancock's paper sufficiently show that you agree with the Council in thinking that some such tribute was due to the memory of our late distinguished fellow-member; and also show that you are of opinion that Dr. Hancock has discharged in an appropriate and graceful manner the task entrusted to him by the Council, and has well expressed the sentiments we must all feel in contemplating so useful and honourable a career as Mr. Thom's.

APPENDIX 10

THOM COLLECTION, NATIONAL MUSEUM OF IRELAND

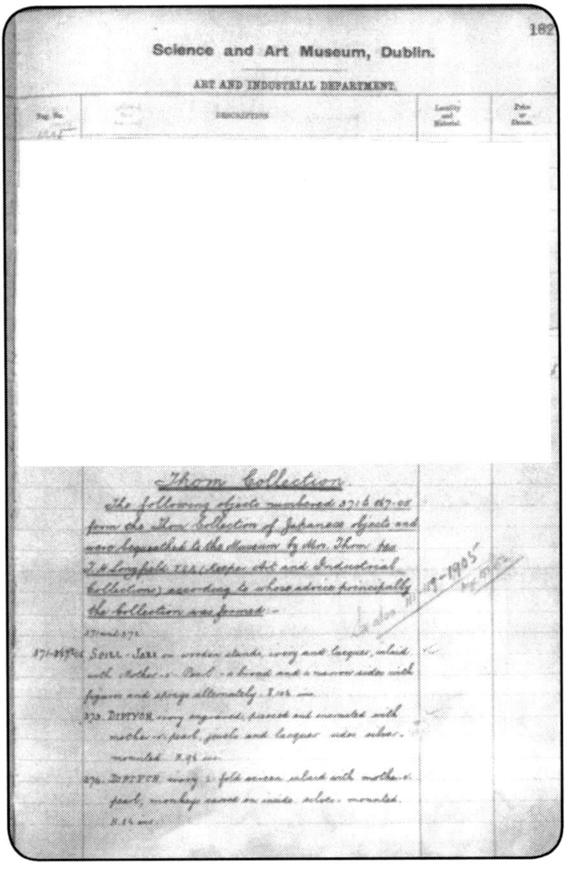

182

Science and Art Museum, Dublin.

ART AND INDUSTRIAL DEPARTMENT.

Thom Collection.

APPENDIX 11

THOM BEQUEST, NATIONAL LIBRARY OF IRELAND

APPENDIX 12

PILKINGTON HISTORY AND PEDIGREES

HARLAND'S

HISTORY AND PEDIGREES OF THE PILKINGTONS,

FROM THE SAXON AND NORMAN TIMES TO THE
PRESENT CENTURY,

COLLECTED FROM THE ANCIENT RECORDS, DEEDS, CHARTERS, &c.

WITH ENGRAVINGS.

WITH TWELVE SHEET PEDIGREES CONTAINING THE
DESCENT FROM THE LORDS OF PILKINGTON, AND
RIVINGTON, TO BRANCHES OF THE PILKINGTONS OF
STAUNTON, YORKSHIRE BARONETS, HALLIWELL,
SHARPLES, AND QUEEN'S CO., BOLTON, PRESTON,
ST. HELENS, WESTMEATH, KILDARE, CAPE TOWN,
AND UNITED STATES.

KIRWAN FAMILY, OF THE GALWAY TRIBES, FROM
THE KINGS OF IRELAND.

ANNOTATIONS OF NEARLY 100 PEERS, &c.,
DESCENDED FROM THE PILKINGTONS.

APPENDIX OF IRISH DEEDS REGISTERED.

FOURTH EDITION.
(Limited to 196 Copies.)

BY

R. G. PILKINGTON, C.S.,

LEGAL ANTIQUARY, MEMBER OF THE ROYAL SOCIETY OF ANTIQUARIES
OF IRELAND.

DUBLIN:

PRINTED BY ALEX. THOM & CO. (LIMITED), 87, 88, & 89, ABBEY St. ....

1906.

[Entered at Stationers' Hall.]

APPENDIX 13

FREDERICK PILKINGTON'S WILL

On 5 February 1897, Frederick wrote his last will and testament, by which time:

Margaret, his eldest daughter, had married John Ormsby, after losing her first husband;

Alexander, his eldest son, had died, survived by Agnes and family;

Frances, his second daughter, had married John Hornidge and had family;

Frederick, his second son, had married Margaret Wilson and had family;

Maria, his third daughter, was aged forty-six and unmarried;

Olivia, his fourth daughter, had married Scrope Rynd, but was aged forty-four and childless;

Hamlet, his third son, had died unmarried;

William, his fourth son, had married Kathleen Richardson and had family;

Edward, his youngest son, was aged thirty-seven and single;

Eveline, his fifth daughter, had married John Lyons and had family;

Violet, his youngest daughter, had married Huband Gregg and had family.

In his will, Frederick was very specific about his intentions.

(1)   He bequeathed to his son Edward Shenton, the lands at Rathbody in the Barony of Ardee, County Meath, but with the condition that before selling that land to others, he must first offer it to his brothers Frederick Coddington and William Handcock successively. If either brother accepted the offer within three months, the price was to be established by two valuers appointed by the two parties, such valuers also appointing an umpire to adjudicate any dispute on price.

(2)   He bequeathed the rest of his real and personal estate to the use of his trustees and executors and administrators for the purposes set out in clauses (3) to (25).

(3)   He bequeathed to his son Frederick Coddington, the sum of £1000 'as a mark of affection for him, my sole reason for not leaving him a large legacy being that he is already through his own ability a wealthy man.'

(4)   He bequeathed in trust for his grandson Lionel, £20,000 'in case he shall become tenant in tail in possession of Newberry Hall and shall attain the age of twenty-six years

or shall marry after my death under that age with the consent of my trustees or trustee for the time being; but if he shall die in my lifetime or shall not attain the age of twenty-six or shall marry without such consent under that age, I bequeath the same in trust for my grandson Lyeth Pilkington.' In the event of both of the sons of Alexander Pilkington defaulting on the above conditions, the £20,000 was to form part of Frederick's residuary estate.

(5) He directed that during the minority of either of his grandsons entitled to Newberry Hall, the executors ensure that the head rent taxes and other outgoings of the property were paid, using if necessary, the interest dividends and annual proceeds of the legacy so bequeathed to him and that the interest of that £20,000 legacy be paid to him from the age of twenty-one, until he attains the age of twenty-six or shall marry.

(6) He directed that the legacy of £20,000 to Lionel or in turn, Lyeth, be conditional on either of them signing within six months of his being entitled to Newberry Hall or attaining the age of twenty-one, whichever occurred last, a bond to Frederick's trustees that he will not, without the consent of the trustees, alter the house buildings or out-offices of Newberry Hall as it now exists or remove any trees, ornamental shrubs, or plantations and that he will not sell or dispose of the residence without first giving the right of pre-emption to successively Frederick Coddington Pilkington, William Handcock Pilkington, and Edward Shenton Pilkington, at a fair and reasonable price determined by two appointed valuers, and if

necessary, an umpire. Further, he directed his trustees not to pay over the legacy until such bond is completed and that in the event the bond is not completed within the stipulated time, the £20,000 be paid to William Handcock Pilkington.

(7) He directed that his trustees and executors hold £4,000 of New South Wales 3.5 per cent inscribed stock (or, if not held at the time of his death, £4,000 cash) upon trust to pay the dividends and income thereof to his daughter Maria Pilkington for as long as she remained unmarried or until she assigned mortgages or parts with the same or any interest therein. In the event of her death or any such event, the aforementioned legacy was to be directed to his son William Handcock Pilkington for his own use and benefit. Further, he empowered his trustees to decide in Maria's interests whether to pay her the dividend direct or to manage and administer such dividend for her clothing, board, lodging, maintenance, and support for her personal and peculiar benefit during spinsterhood, etc. and to decide 'whether she shall be at any time competent or incompetent to give an acquitance for the said moneys'.

(8) As he was desirous for making a further provision for his married daughters and their families in addition to the sums settled upon them when marrying, Frederick directed that the trustees pay to the trustees of the settlement of his daughter Margaret Ormsby, £1,000, the income of which was to be paid to her for her separate use for the duration of her life, after which, the principal was to be held for the benefit of the three daughters

of her first marriage with Robert St John Mayne and shared equally. Additionally, £1,000 was bequeathed to his granddaughter May Woodwright and £2,000 to his granddaughter Aida Mayne. In the event of any of the above-mentioned three granddaughters predeceasing him, the sums above due to that granddaughter were to be shared equally between her surviving descendants.

(9) He bequeathed £1,000 to his daughter Frances Hornidge.

(10) He bequeathed £3,000 to his daughter Olivia Rynd.

(11) He bequeathed £3,000 to his daughter Eveline Maud Lyons.

(12) He bequeathed £5,000 to his daughter Violet Josephine Gregg.

(13) He directed his trustees and executors to retain the legacies bequeathed to his four last-named daughters and to invest same (in securities compatible with their marriage settlements) and pay for life the income thereof 'for their separate use independently of any husbands and without power of anticipation'. Further, upon her death, the capital and income were to be held in trust for the bequest for her issue, in line with her deed or will. In the absence of such deed or will, that legacy was to be divided equally amongst her surviving children.

(14) However, in the case of Eveline Maud Lyons, whose eldest son was already amply provided for, such eldest son or such other son of hers who became entitled to the family estate under her marriage settlement would not, in default of appointment, receive any share of the legacy bequeathed to his mother, but that same would

go to her younger child or be divided equally amongst her younger children.

(15) In the case of his daughter Olivia Rynd, if she were to die without issue, leaving her husband Scrope Rynd her survivor, Frederick's trustees and executors would pay the income of said legacy of £3,000 to his son-in-law for the duration of his natural life. He also authorised his trustees, without risk to them, to loan to Scrope that sum which, in addition to moneys still owed on a loan for the stocking of his land, equates to the £3,000 legacy with his farm at Gortmore, County Westmeath, as security, the same to be served by mortgage repayable on the death of the survivor of Scrope and Olivia.

(16) If any of his said daughters Frances Ball Hornidge, Eveline Maud Lyons, or Violet Josephine Gregg were to die without (surviving) issue, the sum so bequeathed would thereupon form part of the residue of Frederick's personal estate and go accordingly, and that if Olivia Rynd were to die without issue, then after the death of Scrope Rynd, the bequest to Olivia of £3,000 was to be paid to William Handcock Pilkington.

(17) He bequeathed to his son Edward Shenton Pilkington, £9000.

(18) He bequeathed to the male issue of his deceased son, Alexander Pilkington, or such person who would first after Frederick's death be entitled to Newberry Hall and lands and be twenty-one or more years and to William Handcock Pilkington, to share and share alike all the horned stock, sheep, farm horses, farm implements, and all farm produce, also any balance on foot of his Number

2 stock account in the Royal Bank, plate and plated ware which belonged to Frederick at the time of his demise. Further, he directed his trustees to have an inventory of the above made immediately after his demise and valuations made and thereupon divided as they see fit.

(19) He bequeathed to such one of the issue of his deceased son Alexander Pilkington or such person who would first after Frederick's death be entitled to Newberry Hall and be twenty-one years or more, all his pictures, linen, china, glass, and furniture at Newberry Hall.

(20) He bequeathed to his son William Handcock Pilkington, all the furniture at his (Frederick's) house at Haggard.

(21) He bequeathed the residue of his real and personal estate that he owned or over which he had any disposing power, to his son Edward Shenton Pilkington.

(22) He declared it his will and desire that no part of his estate and effects should be sold by public auction.

(23) He decreed that the several legacies previously mentioned may be paid at the direction of his trustees at a valuation, rather than being sold. His executors also were to have full power to apportion and allot such securities to the several legatees based on the market price applicable the day after his death.

(24) He wished that his daughter Maria should live with whichever of his said daughters his trustees and executors shall arrange.

(25) He appointed his son William Handcock Pilkington and his son-in-law John Hornidge executors and trustees of his will and guardians of his daughter Maria. He

left to each of them £100 for their trouble in acting as executors.

Witnesses to the signing of the will by Frederick Pilkington were Joseph Galloway and Joseph William Galloway, solicitors, 55 Upper Sackville Street, Dublin.

On 11 March, 1897, Frederick wrote a codicil to his will, in which:

(26) He revoked the legacy of £20,000 for his grandson Lionel or other the person entitled in tail in possession of Newberry Hall, payable upon attaining the age of twenty-six years. He now gave the sum of £20,000 to his son William Handcock Pilkington and to his son-in-law John Hornidge, 'who and the survivors of them and the executors and administrators of such survivors or other the trustees or trustee of my said will are hereinafter referred to as my trustees upon trust, to invest the same in any securities allowed by law to trustees, or to retain existing securities or investments of my own of the value on the day after my decease of £20,000 and employ the interest dividends and income in the first place during the minority of my grandson Lionel Pilkington in paying the head rent taxes and other outgoings of Newberry Hall, including therein the expenses of all necessary repairs and shall apply the whole or such part as they in their discretion shall think fit of the residue of said interest dividends and income for or towards the maintenance education or benefit for the said Lionel Pilkington until he shall attain twenty-one.' Frederick permitted the

trustees to pay the same to Lionel's mother or guardian for the purpose aforesaid, without their interference on its application; he also decreed that during Lionel's minority, the trustees accumulate and reinvest any surplus.

(27)   He continued to impose on Lionel the bond conditions regarding modifications to, or sale of, Newberry Hall as defined in Clause (6) above.

(28)   He directed that his trustees shall pay the dividends, interest, and income to Lionel until he attains the age of thirty-six, unless and until he marries without the consent of Frederick's trustees or some event happens whereby if that income had belonged to Lionel absolutely, he would be deprived of the personal enjoyment thereof. Further, on Lionel attaining the age of thirty-six, if he had properly executed the above bond and had not married without the consent of the Trustees and had not become bankrupt and not assigned or changed the £20,000 or any part thereof or the income thereof, the trustees were to pay the said £20,000 and accumulations thereof to him as his own absolute property. However, if Lionel dies under twenty-one or dies unmarried between twenty-one and thirty-six years and his brother Lyeth succeeds to Newberry Hall as tenant in tail, then all the above conditions in this codicil shall apply to him. Further, if Lionel did not execute the bond within the required time or before attaining the age of thirty-six, he became bankrupt or assigned or changed the said sum of £20,000, or any part thereof or the income thereof or in the event of both of his grandsons dying unmarried

under the age of thirty-six or in the event of Lionel dying under such age and Lyeth not succeeding as tenant in tail at Newberry Hall, Frederick directed that the £20,000 be directed to William Handcock Pilkington, his executors, administrators, or assigns.

(29) Frederick directed that in the event of Lionel marrying after his death under the age of thirty-six without the consent of his trustees, the said sum of £20,000 shall fall into Frederick's residuary estate.

(30) Frederick authorised his trustees, in the event of Lionel under the age of thirty-six marrying with their consent, in their absolute discretion to settle the £20,000 legacy to Lionel and his wife and family or his intended wife and family, conditional on provisos the trustees see fit to impose.

(31) Frederick now directed that the 50/50 sharing of farm stock between Lionel and William Handcock Pilkington, as per Clause (18) be revised, having regard to the stock requirements of their respective farms, to 2/5 to Lionel and 3/5 to William Handcock Pilkington.

Witnesses to the signing of this first codicil were Thomas Potterton of Ardkill and Patrick Merriman of Derrinturn.

On 29 July 1897, Frederick wrote a second codicil to his will, in which:

(32) He revoked Clause (31) above. On the grounds that (a) he had not opened a No.2 or stock account with the Royal Bank of Ireland, and (b) that the annual cost of stocking his land averages about £5,000, but that the value of the

cattle thereon fluctuates according to the season of the year, he directed that the value of the bequest of horned stock to Lionel shall be deemed to be £2,000, and to his son William Handcock Pilkington be deemed to be £3,000. He further directed that if the value of the cattle on the respective farms left to them is not at the time of Frederick's death equivalent to those amounts, then any shortfall shall be taken from his general personal estate. He empowered his executors, if necessary, to employ competent valuers, whose decisions were binding and conclusive.

Witnesses to the signing of the second codicil were Thomas Potterton, farmer, of Ardkill, and Patrick Merriman, land steward of Derrinturn.

On 9 November 1898, in the Queen's Bench Division (Probate) of the High Court of Justice of Ireland, the last will and two codicils of Frederick Pilkington were proved and registered, and administration of the estate was passed to his executors, William Handcock Pilkington of Haggard and John Hornidge of Calverston, Mullingar. The gross value of the estate within the United Kingdom was £64,861.14s.4d. An officer of Inland Revenue confirmed by signed receipt that estate duty and interest of £4,477.7s.2d. had been paid, the interest being charged at the rate of 5.5 per cent.

APPENDIX 14

FARMING INDENTURE FOR WALTER THOM

Memorandum of an agreement made and entered into the first day of March 1855 between Alexander Thom of Donnycarney House, Esquire, in the County of Dublin and John Bolton of Cullen House in the County of Meath, Esquire.

Whereas the said Alexander Thom is desirous of placing his son Walter Thom (with the consent of the said Walter Thom certified by his signing hereof) with the said John Bolton as a resident pupil for the purpose of acquiring a knowledge of farming and becoming conversant with all matters connected with agricultural pursuits and for the purpose aforesaid, the said Alexander Thom hereby agrees with the said John Bolton as follows:

1.—That the said Walter Thom is to reside and live with the said John Bolton's family and to be treated as such in every respect for a period of two years and six months from the date hereof, and during that time, he is to be provided by the said John Bolton with good and sufficient meals, drink, lodging, and washing befitting him as a resident pupil as aforesaid.

2.—That during the period aforesaid, the said John Bolton is to instruct and teach the said Walter Thom to the best of Mr Bolton's skill and ability in all things appertaining to the business or calling of a farmer and shall in every way in his power aid and assist the said Walter Thom in acquiring such knowledge and information during the term before-mentioned.

3.—That in consideration of the foregoing stipulations on the part of the said John Bolton, the said Alexander Thom hereby agrees for himself his executors, administrators, or assigns to pay or cause to be paid to the said John Bolton the following sums at the several dates following, viz., the sum of £50 Sterling upon the first day of March instant, a further sum of £50 upon the first day of September next, a further sum of £50 upon the first day of March, which will be in the year 1856, a further sum of £50 upon the first day of September next following and a sum of £50 upon the first day of March 1857—the last mentioned date; provided always that in the event of the death of the said Walter Thom or any unforeseen circumstance arising to render the termination of this agreement necessary or desirable sooner than the term hereinbefore specified, the said Alexander Thom shall in such case not be liable to nor be called upon to pay unto the said John Bolton his executors, administrators, or assigns any further sum than he shall already have been paid on the gale day preceding such termination of this agreement.

4.—That during the residence of the said Walter Thom with Mr Bolton as such pupil as aforesaid, the said Walter Thom is to be supplied with clothing, together with medicine and medical advice and attendance, if necessary, at the sole expense and charges of the said Alexander Thom.

We respectively agree to the foregoing conditions and stipulations as witness our hands this third day of March 1855.

Signatory:
Alexander Thom
John Bolton
Walter Thom

Witness:
Henry Senior
J. Brindley

APPENDIX 15

THE EARLY GENERATIONS

Alexander Thom
id. 1.001
b. 1715 Bervie,Kincardine
m. 14.09.1732 Kinneff & Catterline, Kincardine

Margaret Dorward
id. 1.001A
b. 1718 Kinneff & Catterline, Kincardine

    Anne Thom
    id. 2.001
    c. 06.03.1738 Kinneff & Catterline

    Alexander Thom
    id .2.002
    c. 03.01.1742 Barras, Kincardine
    m. 04.06.1763 Bervie, Kincardine
    d. circa 1806 Scotland

    Christian Henderson
    id. 2.002A
    b. circa 1745

        Christian Thom
        id. 3.001
        c. 30.01.1764 Bervie, Scotland

        Alexander Thom
        id. 3.002
        c. 28.02.1766 Bervie, Scotland

        John Thom
        id. 3.003
        c. 30.03.1767 Bervie, Scotland

        James Thom
        id. 3.004
        c. 20.07.1768 Bervie, Scotland

        Walter Thom
        id. 3.005
        b. 14.04.1770 Bervie, Scotland
        m.13.04.1800 Kincardine
        d. 16.06.1824 b'd St Lukes Dublin

        Margaret Turner
        id. 3.005A
        b. 06.05.1770 Ellon, Scotland
        d. 04.05.1842 b'd St Luke's Dublin

            Alexander Thom
            id. 4.001
            b. 18.04.1801 Bervie, Scotland
            m. 07.07.1824 Dublin, Ireland

            m. 16.05.1870 Edinburgh, Scotland
            d. 22.12.1879 b'd Mt Jerome, Dublin

            Maria Dillon
            id. 4.001A
            b. dd.mm.1797 Ireland
            d. 18.03.1867 b'd Mt Jerome Dublin.

            Sarah Mackay (nee McCulloch)
            id. 4.001B
            b. 1820
            d. 20.09.1903 b'd Mt Jerome. Dublin

                William Lindsay Mackay
                id. 5.010 Stepson to Alexander
                b. circa 1851, Ireland
                d.19.04.1903 b'd Mt Jerome, Dublin

          Margaret Thom
          id. 5.001
          b. dd.09.1825 Dublin, Ireland

                Continued Appendix 16

          Walter Thom
          id. 5.002
          c. 27.09.1826 Dublin, Ireland

          Patrick Thom
          id. 5.003
          b. dd. 07.1828 Dublin, Ireland
          m. 07.06.1854 Dublin, Ireland
          d. b'd 08.02.1871 Isle of Man

          Sidney Thornburgh Browne
          id. 5.003A

              Sidney Frances Thornburgh Thom
              id. 6.015
              b. 1869
              d. b'd 16.12.1870 Braddan, Isle of Man

          Robert Thom
          id. 5.004
          c. 04.06.1830 Dublin, Ireland

Alexander Thom
id. 5.005
c. 07.01.1833 Dublin, Ireland

Maria Thom
id. 5.006
b. dd.01.1834 Dublin, Ireland
d. 11.03.1903 b'd Mt Jerome, Dublin.

Walter Thom
id. 5.007
b. dd.05.1835 Dublin, Ireland

Continued Appendix 17

Robert Thom
id. 5.008
b. 06.05.1837 Dublin, Ireland
m. 01.03.1871 Geelong Vic
d. 25.07.1892. b'd Portarlington Vic

Annie Cox
id. 5.008A
b. 09.03.1853 Chilwell, Vic

Victoria Maria Annie Dillon Thom
id. 6.019
b. 29.01.1873 North Paywit, Vic
d. 21.08.1887, Geelong, Vic

Alice Margaret Kathleen Eva Thom
id. 6.022
b. 28.09.1874 North Paywit, Vic
d. 14.10.1908 Ballarat, Vic

Fanny Alberta Cora Jane Thom
id. 6.024
b. 08.10.1876 North Paywit, Vic

Continued Appendix 19

Albert Charles Alexander Robert Thom
id. 6.026
b. 28.05.1878 North Paywit, Vic
m.22.04.1914 Geelong, Vic
d. 13.10.1918 b'd Rouen, France

Elizabeth Gray
id. 6.026A
b. 1889 Fairfield, Vic

William Nathaniel Walter Hamlet Thom
id. 6.027
b. 08.11.1880 St Leonards, Vic
d. 20.02.1881 Sandridge. Vic

William Nathaniel Walter Hamlet Thom
id. 6.028
b. 11.12.1881 St Leonards Vic

Continued Appendix 20

Mabel Beatrice Louisa Jane Thom
id. 6.029
b. 08.05.1885 St Leonards Vic

Continued Appendix 21

Victoria Jane Thom
id. 5.009
b. dd.09.1838 Dublin, Ireland
d. 29.03.1914. b'd Mt Jerome, Dublin

Elizabeth Helen Thom
id. 4.002
b. 25.07.1802 Bervie, Scotland
d. 10.03.1803 b'd Bervie, Scotland

Elizabeth Helen Thom
id. 4.003
b. 02.04.1804 Bervie, Scotland
d. 02.03.1805 b'd Bervie Scotland

Jean Thom
id. 4.004
b. 14.03.1806 Bervie, Scotland
d. 15.07.1832 Dublin

Jean Thom
id. 3.006
c. 08.05.1773 Bervie, Scotland

APPENDIX 16

THE PILKINGTONS

Margaret Thom
id. 5.001
b. dd.09.1825 Dublin, Ireland
m. 29.08.1844 Dublin, Ireland
d. 23.08.1878 b'd Carbury, Kildare.

Frederick Pilkington
id.5.001A
b. 1820 Ireland
d. 19.05.1898 b'd Carbury, Kildare

    Margaret Elizabeth Pilkington
    id. 6.001
    b. 1845 Dublin
    m. 08.06.1865 Carbury, Kildare

    Robert St John Mayne
    id. 6.001A
    b. 24.06.1843 Dublin, Ireland
    d. 1874 Dublin

        Aida Constance Mayne
        id. 7.001.
        b. 04.05.1868 Dublin
        m. 14.01.1905 Dublin

        Arthur Forde Pilson
        id. 7.001
        b. 17.05.1865 Downpatrick, Co. Down.

        Florence Ethel Mayne
        id. 7.002
        b. 27.07.1869 Dublin
        m. 14.10.1892 Carbury, Co. Kildare

        Smith Ramadge Ramadge
        id. 7.002A

        m. 22.04.1899 Dublin, Ireland

        John Hall
        id. 7.002B

        May Josephine Sedborough Mayne
        id. 7.003
        b. circa 1871
        m. 14.10.1892 Carbury, Co. Kildare
        d. 19.03.1928 Bournemouth, England

        William Henry Edward Woodwright
        id. 7.003A
        b. 10.07.1865 Ballybay, Co. Monaghan, Ireland

    m.18.05.1875, Dublin
    d. Q1, 1923 Dublin

    John Arthur Cooper Ormsby
    id. 6.001B
    b. 1843 Sligo, Ireland
    d. xx.06.1922 Dublin

        Arabella Mabel Nicholson Ormsby
        id.7.006
        b. 07.05.1876 Dublin
        m.17.06.1905 Dublin
        d. 1957

        Ralph Smith Oliver Cusack
        id.7.006A
        b. 21.12.1875 Dublin, Ireland
        d. 1965

        Margaret Muriel Ormsby
        id 7.011
        b. 08.09.1880 Kildare

Alexander Pilkington
id. 6.002
b. 30.06.1846 Carbury, Kildare
m. 1875 Dublin, Ireland
d. 10.03.1887. b'd Carbury, Kildare

Agnes Mayhew
id.6.002A
b. 11.07.1854 London, England
d. 14.02.1925 b'd Carbury, Kildare

    Edith Pilkington
    id. 7.009
    b. 22.07.1878 Dublin

    Lionel Pilkington
    id.7.010
    b. 30.03.1880 Carbury. Co Kildare
    m.05.05.1916 Tasmania Australia
    d. 21.09.1967 Dublin, Ireland

    Bertha Harriet Maud Stephens
    id. 7.010A
    b. circa 1888
    d. 1962 Ivanhoe, Vic

        Joyce Eileen Pilkington
        id. 8.006
        b. 15.06.1918 Launceston, Tasmania

    Lyulph Frederick Pilkington
    id. 7.013
    b. Q1, 1883 Dublin, Ireland

    Florence Pilkington
    id. 7.016
    b. Q2, 1884 Kildare, Ireland

Frances Ball Pilkington
id. 6.003
b. circa 1848
m. 11.12.1872 Dublin
d. Q2, 1923 Dublin

John Hornidge
id. 6.003A
b. 30.11.1841
d. 06.03.1902 Mullingar, Westmeath, Ireland

    Sybil Pilkington Hornidge
    id. 7.004
    b. 19.09.1873 Carbury, Kildare
    d. Q3, 1957 Dublin

    Olive Hilda Beatrice Pilkington Hornidge
    id. 7.008
    b. 22.11.1877 Edenderry, Offaly, Ireland
    m. 14.10.1903 Dublin

    James Campbell
    id. 7.008A
    b. Sligo, Ireland
    d. 1920s

    m.
    d. 06.03.1939

    James Berry
    id. 7.008B
    b. Newcastle, Co Down

Bervie and Beyond

Dudley George Pilkington Hornidge
id. 7.012
b. 29.09.1881 Mullingar, Westmeath
m. 15.09.1909 Banbridge, Down, NI
d. 02.06.1954 Mullingar, Westmeath

Kathleen Anne Harden
id. 7.012A
b. Q1,1883, Armagh, Ireland
d. 10.09.1946 Mullingar, Westmeath

John Dudley Hornidge
id. 8.001
b. 23.06.1910 Mullingar, Westmeath
m. 20.03.1945 Glasgow, Scotland
d. 16.12.1990 Mullingar, Westmeath

Helen Lorraine Steel Blair
id. 8.001A
b. 16.06.1922 Glasgow, Scotland

Susan Lorraine Hornidge
id. 9.007
b. 28.11.1946
m. 1978

Michael Alexander Stephens
id. 9.007A

Catherine Alexandra Stephens
id.10.017
b 1980

Belinda Stephens
id. 10.020
b. 1981

Carol Heather Hornidge
id.9.010
b. 22.02.1949 Mullingar, Westmeath
m.

Carlos de la Flor
id. 9.010A

David de la Flor
id. 10.003
b. 1970

Victor de la Flor
id. 10.006
b. 1973

Daniel de la flor
id. 10.009
b. 1975

m.

David Elling
id. 9.010B
d. 07.09.2008

Gail Priscilla Hornidge
id. 9.016
b. 28.12.1952
m. 1977

John Richard Jenner
id. 9.016A

Thomas Robert Jenner
id. 10.015
b. 1979
m. 22.06.2011

Sarbjit Kaur Sandhu
id.10.015A

Edward Jenner
id. 10.025
b. 1982

Gillian Rona Hornidge
id. 9.033
b. 1959
m.

Simon
id. 9.033A

m.

Malcolm Wilkes
id. 9.033B

Pamela Marjery Hornidge
id. 8.005
b. 29.12.1915 Dublin, Ireland
m. 07.02.1948 USA

Carl Edwin Bjorlin
id. 8.005A
b. 17.07.1917 New York USA
d. 03.02.2002 New York, USA

Charles Dudley Bjorlin
id. 9.013
b. 04.11.1951 New York, USA
d. 25.11.1995 USA

Eric Stephen Bjorlin
id. 9.018
b. 29.10.1953 New York, USA

Hannelore Mentzel
id. 9.018A
b. 01.06.1949 East Germany

Denis Richard Hornidge
id. 8.007
b. 26.07.1918 Dublin, Ireland
m. 15.02.1942 London England
d. 24.10.2007 Farnham, England

Millicent Lilias Yelverton Dawson
id. 8.007A
b. 31.10.1921 St Peter Port, Channel Islands
d. 26.10.1987 Farnham, England

Alvis Robb
id. 8.007B
d. 1999

Deirdre Lidderdale Hornidge
id. 9.003
b. 05.10.1943 London, England
m. 05.08.1967 Farnham, England

David John Knowler
id. 9.003A
b. 20.06.1943 Farnham, England

Meredith Jane Knowler
id. 10.005
b. 21.11.1972 Adelaide, Australia

James Robin Knowler
id. 10.010
b. 29.01.1975 Adelaide, Australia

m. 20.12.1986 Adelaide, Australia

Robert Wayne Schahinger
id. 9.003B
b. 27.10.1948 Adelaide, Australia

Aileen Felicity Hornidge
id. 9.006
b. 26.08.1946 Farnham, England
m.28.04.1966 Dumfries, Scotland

Bryan Donald Needham
id. 9.006A
b. 17.03.1942 Stirling Scotland

Emma Peta Needham
id. 10.001
b. 28.06.1966 London, England
m. 29.03.2006 Kalkan, Turkey

Ozcan Turk
id. 10.001A
b. 14.06.1978 Manavgat, Turkey

Aileen Besire Turk
id. 11.015
b. 26.12.2007 Frimley, England

Natalie Mercedese Needham
id. 10.002
b. 19.03.1968 London, England
m. 30.07.1994 Farnham, England

Thomas Fulton (b. Thomas Reid)
id. 10.002A
b. 01.01.1967 Glasgow, Scotland

Oliver Reid Fulton
id. 11.003
b. 21.08.1998 Guidford, England

Jack Bryan Fulton
id. 11.005
b. 17.03.2000 Guildford, England

Thomas Alexander Fulton
id. 11.006.
b. 17.03.2000 Guildford, England

Bryony Rose Needham
id. 10.026
b. 02.01.1982 Frimley, England
m.26.06.2009 Winchfield, England

Mark John Ormond
id. 10.026A
b. 05.02.1981 Fleetwood, England

Fredrick Richard Ormond
id. 11.025
b. 23.06.2011 Kingston upon Thames, England

Jennifer Francis Lilias Hornidge
id. 9.015
b. 27.03.1952 Kitwe, Zambia
m.16.08.1975 Farnham, England

John Campbell Wyper
id. 9.015A
b. 09.12.1948 Motherwell, Scotland

Siobhan Lilias Wyper
id. 10.019
b. 23.10.1980 Frimley, England
m.19.08.2004 Farnham, England

Jorge Mata Gonzales
id. 10.019A
b. 29.10.1977 Oviedo, Spain

Daniel Mata Gonzales
id. 11.017
b. 09.09.2008 Madrid, Spain

Robin Mata Gonzales
id. 11.023
b. 09.10.2010 Madrid, Spain

Lauren Hornidge Wyper
id. 10.030
b. 06.08.1984 Muscat, Oman
m.16.11.2011 Edinburgh, Scotland

Neil Halliday
id. 10.030A
b. 13.01.1985 Airdrie, Scotland.

Guy Mulock Pilkington Hornidge
id. 7.015
b. 13.04.1884 Mullingar, Westmeath
m. 05.10.1912

Flora Pearson
id. 7.015A
d. xx.07.1913 Reading, England

Patrick Rowan Hornidge
id. 8.002
b. 15.07.1913
m. 04.05.1940

Angela Inez Santos
id. 8.002A
d. 1952

Veronica Geraldine Hornidge
id. 9.001
b. 22.06.1941

Vanessa Hornidge
id. 9.002
b. 17.01.1943

Christopher Rowan Hornidge
id. 9,004
b. 01.12.1944

m.   **Sheila XXX**
           id. 8.002B

m. 19.09.1927   **Beatrice Thirza Sparks**
d. 29.06.1953 Malaya   id. 7.015B

Brian Guy Hornidge
id. 8.015
b. 15.06.1928

Sheilagh Mary Hornidge   **Martin Braun**
id. 8.017   id. 8.017A
b. 24.11.1929
d. 1997

Nicholas Braun
id. 9.014

Caroline Braun
id. 9.019

Frederick Coddington Pilkington   **Margaret Louisa Wilson**
id. 6.004   id. 6.004A
b. 1849 Carbury, Kildare   b. circa 1853 Lissidian, Armagh, Ireland
m.1872 Rathdown, Dublin, Ireland
d. 27.01.1924 London, England

Frederick Ernest Chomley Pilkington
id. 7.005
b. 08.10.1873 Stillorgan, Dublin
d. 06.10.1901 Vryheid, Sth Africa

Mina Olive Pilkington
id. 7.007
b. 1877 Rathdown, Dublin

Maria Pilkington
id. 6.005
b. circa 1851 Carbury, Kildare

Olivia Wade Pilkington   **Scrope Bernard Christopher Rynd**
id. 6.006   id. 6.006A
b.circa 1853, Carbury, Kildare   b. circa 1848, Dublin
m. 25.02.1875 Dublin.   d. Q3, 1907 Ballymahon, Longford, Ireland

Hamlet Wade Pilkington
id. 6.007
b.1854 Carbury, Kildare
d. 10.11.1886 Edenderry, Offaly, Ireland

William Handcock Pilkington   **Kathleen Richardson**
id. 6.008   id. 6.008A
b. 1859 Carbury, Kildare   b.31.07.1867 Rock Ferry, Cheshire, England
m.23.11.1887 Toxteth Pk, Lancs, England.   d. 1957 Middlesex, England
d. 23.06.1905 Carbury, Kildare

Frederick Mervyn Fosbery Pilkington   **Bertha Charlotte Georgina Bryan**
id. 7.019   id. 7.019A
b. Q4, 1888 Dublin, Ireland   b. 1891 Enniscorthy, Wexford, Ireland
m .Q1,1914 Dublin, Ireland   d. After 1921.

m. dd.03.1925 London, England   **Ursula Marian Oxenford**
d. 22.07.1940 Staines, Middlesex, England   id. 7.019B
                                       b.15.04.1902 London, England
                                       d. xx.10.1994 Surrey, England

Edward Shenton Pilkington
id. 6.009
b.circa 1861 Carbury, Kildare
d. 14.05.1912 Geelong, Vic

Eveline Maud Pilkington
id.6.010
b. circa 1862 Carbury, Kildare
m. 29.11.1882 Dublin, Ireland

John Charles Lyons
id. 6.010A
b.01.02.1861 Ledestown, Westmeath
d. 1908

John Charles Geoffrey Pilkington Lyons
id. 7.014
b. 17.11.1883 Mullingar, Westmeath, Ireland
m. 1914 Dublin, Ireland

Gladys Maude Pilkington Lyons
id. 7.018
b. 14.06.1887 Westmeath

Coral Cecil Constance Lyons
id. 7.020
b. 27.09.1889 Dublin

Violet Josephine Pilkington
id. 6.011
b. 16.12.1864 Carbury, Kildare
m.05.08.1885 Dublin, Ireland
d. 03.12.1947

Huband George Gregg
id. 6.011A
b. xx.02.1847 Longford, Ireland
d. xx.05.1941

William Thornton Huband Gregg
id. 7.017
b. 12.07.1886, Longford, Ireland
m. 25.10.1919

Frances Lyndall Schreiner
id. 7.017A

Margaret Vivienne Lyndall Gregg
id. 8.008
b. 24.07.1920
m. 31.01.1942

John Augustine Ogilvy
id. 8.008A

Angus William Ogilvy
id. 9.005
b. 06.03.1945

Diana Lyndall Ogilvy
id. 9.008
b. 02.12.1946

Olive Schreiner Gregg
id. 8.012
b. 07.03.1925

Frances Lyndall De Savoie Gregg
id. 8.016
b. 24.08.1929

Hamlet Pilkington Huband Gregg
id. 7.021
b. 17.05.1890 Longford, Ireland
m. 11.08.1913

Florence Mae Schreffler
id. 7.021A

Huband Thornton Raymond Gregg
id, 8.004
b. 21.08.1915
m. 22.11.1945

Beverley Prescott
id. 8.004A

Anthony Thornton Fraser Gregg
id. 9.009
b. 31.01.1947

Timothy Charles William Gregg
id.9.011 Adopted
b. 25.06.1949

Violet Pilkington Huband Gregg
id. 7.022
b. 22.03.1893 Longford, Ireland
m. 31.01.1912 Rathdown, Dublin

Richard William Rice Jeudwine
id. 7.022A
d.31.12.1956

XXX (Male) Jeudwine
id. 8.003

m. 03.03 1928

Ralph Hanham Skrine
id. 7.022B
d. 09.08.1949

Joseph Gregg
id. 7.026
b.Q4,1900 Longford, Ireland
d.Q4,1900 Longford, Ireland

APPENDIX 17

WALTER OF CULLEN

Walter Thom
id. 5.007
b. dd.05.1835 Dublin, Ireland
m.06.04.1864 Dublin, Ireland
d. 24.12.1909 b'd Mt Jerome, Dublin

Mary Ann Ruxton Bolton
id. 5.007A
b.circa 1838
d. 1921. b'd Mt Jerome, Dublin

    Alexander Thom
    id. 6.012
    b. 07.03.1865 Drumcondra, Dublin
    m.29.06.1910 Dublin, Ireland
    d. 14.12.1951 b'd Slane, Meath, Ireland

    Sarah Paine Murphy
    id. 6.012A
    b. 15.02.1881 Ballycullane, Wexford, Ireland
    d. 28.01.1953 b'd Slane,Meath, Ireland

        Sarah Watson Thom
        id. 7.040
        b. 23.04.1918 Reitz, Sth Africa
        m.24.04.1940 Slane, Meath, Ireland
        d. 22.06.1999 b'd Slane, Meath, Ireland

        Herbert John Reid Henderson
        id. 7.040A
        b. 28.11.1914 Oldcastle, N Ireland.
        d. 30.11.1989 b'd Slane, Meath, Ireland

            Alexander Thomas Stephen Henderson
            id. 8.042
            b. 02.04.1943 Dublin, Ireland
            m.15.02.1971 Norwich, England

            Susan Jane Taylor
            id. 8.042A
            b.23.05.1946 Stoke-on-Trent, England

                Trucie Sarah Henderson
                id. 9.080
                b. 28.02.1972 Norwich, England
                m.19.05.2012 Somerset, England

                Edward Anthony Julian Simon Mitchell
                id. 9.080A
                b. 05.02.1972 London, UK.

                Shan William Henderson
                id. 9.090
                b. 03.01.1974 Norwich, England
                m.03.09.2005 Michelmersh, England

                Tamzin Sylvester
                id. 9.090A
                b.18.03.1975 Romsey, England

                    Beatrice Rose Henderson
                    id. 10.145
                    b. 24.11.2007 Salisbury, England

                    Colette Belle Henderson
                    id. 10.153
                    b. 16.06.2010 Salisbury, England

                Mara Jane Henderson
                id. 9.100
                b. 02.04.1976 Wegberg W.Germany
                m.18.11.2011 Norfolk, England

                Carl Ginger
                id. 9.100A

                Dana Siobhan Henderson
                id. 9.110
                b. 18.08.1981 Bury St Edmunds, England

            John Watson Reid Henderson
            id. 8.050
            b. 02.05.1947 Dublin, Ireland

            Hazel Sarah Henderson
            id. 8.052
            b. 11.07.1948 Dublin
            m. 02.06.1973 Slane, Meath, Ireland

            Richard Andrew Spencer
            id. 8.052A
            b.1948 Mansfield, Notts, England

                Emma Spencer
                id. 9.098
                b. 14.12.1975 Kirkaldy, Scotland
                m.09.05.2009

                xxx Key
                id. 9.098A

                Helen Elizabeth Sarah Spencer
                id. 9.108
                b. 29.08.1979 Wegberg, W.Germany

Walter Thom
id. 6.013
b. xx.01.1866 Drumcondra, Ireland
d. 04.01.1886 b'd Mt Jerome, Dublin

Dillon Turner Thom
id. 6.014
b. 03.01.1868 Drumcondra, Dublin
m.02.11.1898 Dublin, Ireland

m.05.06.1935 Dublin, Ireland
d. 18.10.1957 b'd Deansgrange, Dublin

Mary Evelyn d'Bentley
id.6.014A
b. 26.07.1867 Bridgetown, Clare, Ireland
d. 03.02.1934 b'd Mt Jerome, Dublin, Ireland

Evelyn Constance Russell
id. 6.014B
b. Q1,1888 Ballymahon, Longford, Ireland
d. 05.01.1952 b'd Deansgrange, Dublin

Henry Bentley Thom
id.7.025
b. 06.11.1899 Kimberley, Sth Africa
d. 04.05.1926 b'd Mt Jerome, Dublin

Walter Dillon Thom
id. 7.027
b. 26.05.1902 Dublin Ireland

Continued Appendix 18

Alexander Seward Dillon Thom
id. 7.028
b. 06.04.1903 Dublin, Ireland
m. 18.10.1933 Dublin, Ireland

m. 10.11.1954 Dublin, Ireland
d. 25.07.1986 b'd Enniskerry, Wicklow

Doris Hilary Wright
id. 7.028A
b.
d. dd.10.1953 b'd Enniskerry, Wicklow, Ireland

Caroline Rhys Robertson Maunsell
id. 7.028B
b. Q4, 1907 Rathdown, Dublin, Ireland
d. 08.01.1974 b'd Deansgrange, Dublin, Ireland

Bolton Dillon Thom
id. 7.031
b. 31.03.1906 Dublin, Ireland
m.18.08.1934 Dublin, Ireland
d. 11.01.1982 b'd Deansgrange, Ireland

Wilhelmina Margaret Gorman
id. 7.031A
b. 28.05.1906 Dublin, Ireland
d. 26.10.1959 b'd Deansgrange, Ireland

Margaret Evelyn Thom
id. 8.027
b. 03.05.1935 Dublin, Ireland
m.24.10.1959 Glenageary, Dublin, Ireland

Donald MacLean Denton
id. 8.027A
b. 20.07.1931 Ilford,England

Clive Anthony MacLean Denton
id. 9.044
b. 16.03.1962 Sale, Cheshire, England
m.18.10.1999 Tunbridge Wells, England

Laurence France Lerault
id. 9.044A
b. 10.06.1965 Craponne sur Arzon, France

Julien Georges-Henri Soitel
id. 10.079 Stepson to Clive
b. 18.12.1993 Lyon, France

Bertrand Jean-Francois Soitel
id. 10.089 Stepson to Clive
b. 18.12.1995 Lyon, France

Antoine Henri Donald Denton
id. 10.106
b. 10.03.2000 Marseilles, France

Susan Nicola Denton
id. 9.052
b. 18.02.1964 Sale, Cheshire, England
m.08.10.1994 Sissinghurst, England

Richard James Wood
id. 9.052A
b. 15.07.1965 Crawley, England

Alasdair Keith Wood
id. 10.110
b. 09.10.2000 Maidstone England

Georgia Grace Wood
id. 10.116
b. 20.12.2002 Maidstone, England

Geoffrey Bolton Denton
id. 9.062
b. 03.11.1966 Singapore
m. 2004 Gaborone, Africa

Susanne Wonfor
id. 9.062A
b. 02.03.1973 Ipswich, England

Harvey Donald Anthony Denton
id. 10.123
b. 24.02.2004 Gaborone, Botswana

Rosie Anne Margaret Denton
id. 10.133
b. 25.08.2005 Bury St Edmunds, England

Barbara Dillon Thom
id. 8.036
b. 20.06.1938 Dublin, Ireland
m. 23.04.1960 Dublin, Ireland

Michael Robert Lambart Barrett
id. 8.036A
b. 21.10.1935 Dublin, Ireland

David Robert Lambart Barrett
id. 9.039
b. 02.02.1961 Dublin, Ireland
m. 24.03.1990 Stowe, England

Alison Jane Whittington
id. 9.039A
b. 20.02.1959 Bicester, England

Alexander James Barrett
id. 10.059
b. 08.05.1991 London, England

Clemency Sophie Barrett
id. 10.082
b. 20.10.1994 London, England

Jacquelyn Susan Lambart Barrett
id. 9.046
b. 28.03.1963 Dublin, Ireland
m. 24.06.1993 Bedford, England

Issa Farhoud
id. 9.046A
b. 18.02.1961 Beirut, Lebanon

Zayneb Issa Farhoud
id. 10.092
b. 08.05.1996 Bedford, England

Aziza Issa Farhoud
id. 10.100
b. 16.03.1998 Bedford, England

Fairuz Issa Farhoud
id. 10.105
b. 12.08.1999 Bedford, England

Nicola Marjorie Lambart Barrett
id. 9.056
b. 02.09.1965 Dublin, Ireland
m. 06.07.1991 Monkstown, Dublin, Eire

David Edgar McConnell
id. 9.056A
b. 18.09.1964 Dublin, Ireland

Christopher David McConnell
id. 10.096
b. 29.01.1997 Dublin, Ireland

Kate Aoife McConnell
id. 10.102
b. 27.08.1998 Dublin, Ireland

Rosemary Constance Thom
id. 8.040
b. 30.04.1942 Dublin, Ireland
m. 28.03.1970 Dublin, Ireland

Robert Hugh Ivan Coffey
id. 8.040A
b. 19.08.1938 Newtownards, N Ireland

Clare Wilha Coffey
id. 9.076
b. 02.07.1971 Belfast, N Ireland
m.29.10.2001 Belfast, N Ireland

Andrew Roger Gorman
id. 9.076A
b 07.10.1968 Bangor, N Ireland

Natasha Rose Ann Gorman
id. 10.124
b. 24.02.2004 Livingstown, Scotland

Stella Kate Gorman
id. 10.135
b. 20.10.2005 Dumfries, Scotland

Alison Rosemary Coffey
id. 9.094
b. 21.09.1974 Belfast, N Ireland

Hilary Doris Thom
id. 8.045
b. 20.12.1944 Dublin, Ireland
m. 24.09.1971 Glenageary, Dublin

Maurice John Brooks
id. 8.045A
b. 30.04.1942 Dublin, Ireland

Caroline Elizabeth Brooks
id. 9.086
b. 23.05.1973 Dublin, Ireland
m.23.12. 2002 Dublin, Ireland

Paul Edgar Ritchie
id. 9.086A
b.26.10.1972 Cork, Cork, Ireland

Anya Minnie Elizabeth Ritchie
id. 10.126
b. 30.06.2004 Craigavon, N Ireland

Ronan Ed Mossie Ritchie
id. 10.138
b. 25.06.2006 Craigavon, N Ireland

Sian Hilary Rebecca Ritchie
id. 10.150
b. 14.03.2009 Craigavon, N Ireland

Gillian Hazel Brooks
id. 9.096
b. 21.06.1975 Dublin, Ireland
m.20.04.2002 Dublin, Ireland

Ryan Steven Foster
id. 9.096A
b.16.10.1969 Nottingham, England

Lily Rose Foster
id. 10.125
b. 23.06.2004 Nottingham, England

Marla Jade Foster
id. 10.136
b.10.12.2005 Nottingham, England

Adam Anthony Foster
id. 10.142
b. 09.06.2007 Belfast, N Ireland

Joanna Hilary Brooks
id. 9.112
b. 30.11.1982 Dublin, Ireland

Ytang Morcillo Albiol
id. 9.112A
b. 17.10.1979 Castellon, Spain

Robyn Alejandra Morcillo Brooks
id. 10.147
b. 11.06.2008 Madrid, Spain

Leo Ytang Morcillo Brooks
id.10.156
b. 06.04.2012 Dublin, Ireland

Maria Victoria Elizabeth Thom
id. 6.016
b. 18.03.1869 Drumcondra, Dublin, Ireland
d. 12.05.1910 b'd Mt Jerome, Dublin

Robert Thom
id. 6.017
b. circa 1870 Drumcondra, Dublin, Ireland
d. Isle of Wight, England

Sarah Thom
id. 6.018
b. 10.09.1871 Rathfarnham, Dublin, Ireland
d. 1873 b'd Mt Jerome, Dublin

John Bolton Ruxton Thom
id. 6.020
b. 28.03.1873 Rathmines, Dublin, Ireland
d. 13.11.1890 b'd St Helier, Jersey, England.

Frederick Pilkington Thom
id. 6.021
b. 16.07.1874 Dublin, Ireland
d. 05.09.1874 b'd Mt Jerome, Dublin

Hubert Ernest Thom
id. 6.023
b. 07.09.1875 Dublin, Ireland
d. b'd 05.10.1875 Mt Jerome, Dublin

Frederick Robert Thom
id. 6.025
b. 11.04.1877 Drumcondra, Ireland
d. 28.12.1933 Killucan, Westmeath, Ireland

APPENDIX 18

WALTER DILLON OF ARGENTINA

Walter Dillon Thom
id. 7.027
b. 26.05.1902 Dublin Ireland
m. 17.02.1926 Las Palmas,Chaco, Arg'tna.
d. 26.09.1965 b'd Buenos Aires, Argentina

Daphne King
id. 7.027A
b. 17.12.1904 Las Palmas, Argentina
d. 17.05.1946 Buenos Aires, Argentina

    Henry Edward DillonThom
    id.8.013
    b. 07.10.1926 Chaco, Argentina
    m. 09.04.1959 Mercedes, Argentina
    d. 29.03.2003 Mercedes, Argentina

    Aurora Del Carmen Vargas
    id. 8.013A
    b. 24.02.1932 Mercedes, Argentina

        Monica Patricia Thom
        id.9.038
        b. 28.08.1960 Mercedes, Argentina

        Alexander Edward Dillon Thom
        id. 9.042
        b. 03.08.1961 Mercedes, Argentina

        Sylvia Daphne Thom
        id.9.051
        b. 23.12.1963 Mercedes, Argentina
        d. 09.09.1995 Mercedes, Argentina

    Daphne Evelyn Patricia Thom
    id. 8.020
    b. 23.04.1932 San Miguel, Argentina
    m. 23.02.1952 Buenos Aires, Argentina

    Robert Weare Sword
    id. 8.020A
    b. 27.07.1924 England
    d. 25.09.2012 Entre Rios, Argentina

        Rupert Robert Sword
        id. 9.017
        b. 03.01.1953 Buenos Aires, Argentina
        m. 05.08.1978 Dyrham, Glos., England

        Jane Elspeth Summerill
        id. 9.017A
        b. 01.02.1953 Bristol, England

            James Robert William Sword
            id. 10.032
            b. 15.12.1984 London, England
            d. 22.11.1994 Buenos Aires, Argentina

            Juliet Vanessa Sword
            id. 10.056
            b. 04.07.1990 Buenos Aires, Argentina

        Marie Louise Sword
        id. 9.021
        b. 16.11.1954 Concordia, Argentina
        m.15.12.1972 Buenos Aires, Argentina

        Carlos Alberto Matarazzo
        id. 9.021A
        b. 02.02.1942 Buenos Aires, Argentina

        m. 1992 Buenos Aires, Argentina

        Oscar Spinoza Melo
        id. 9.021B

            Roberto Nicolas Matarazzo
            id. 10.007
            b. 28.05.1974 Buenos Aires, Argentina
            m. 04.12.2009 Buenos Aires, Argentina

            Carolina Mintz Olesker
            id. 10.007A
            b. 02.03.1972 Sao Paulo, Brazil

                Clara Matarazzo Mintz
                id. 11.016
                b. 30.03.2008 Buenos Aires, Argentina

                Nicolas Matarazzo Mintz
                id.11.026
                b. 01.02.2012 Buenos Aires, Argentina

APPENDIX 19

FANNY HENDERSON OF AUSTRALIA

Fanny Alberta Cora Jane Thom
id. 6.024
b. 08.10.1876 North Paywit, Vic
m.18.09.1896 Melbourne, Vic
d. 10.09.1961 b'd Fawkner, Vic

William John Henderson
id. 6.024A
b. 30.08.1872 Lal Lal, Vic
d. 21.04.1951 b'd Fawkner, Vic

    Holly Lavinia Eileen Henderson
    id. 7.023
    b. 03.01.1897 Curlewis, Vic
    m. 27.04.1920 Allambie, Vic
    d. 23.05.1985 b'd Dandenong, Vic

    Thomas Budd
    id. 7.023A
    b. 03.07.1888 Stokes Bliss, UK
    d. 07.03.1971 b'd Springvale, Vic

        Charles Thomas Budd
        id. 8.009
        b. 23.06.1921 Warragul, Vic
        m. 06.12.1947 Camberwell, Vic
        d. 05.05.2004 Neeram Sth, Vic

        Nancy May Howrit
        id. 8.009A
        b. 08.07.1924
        d. 2003 Warragul, Vic

        Albert Raymond Budd
        id. 8.010
        b. 1924 Warragul, Vic
        d. 1981 b'd Dandenong, Vic

        Fay Plant
        id. 8.010A

            Trevor Budd
            id. 9.012

        Clova Muriel Daphne Budd
        id. 8.011
        b. 1925
        d. 1925 Yarragon, Vic

        Kathleen Aileen May Budd
        id. 8.014
        b. 05.05.1928 Warragul, Vic
        m. 08.11.1947 Brunswick, Vic

        Reginald Alfred Williams
        id. 8.014A
        b. 24.01.1905 Bradford, England
        d. 13.09.1986 Canterbury, Vic

            Andrew Norman Williams
            id. 9.022
            b. dd.mm. 1956 Melbourne. Vic
            d. dd.mm.1956 Melbourne, Vic

            Michael Anthony Williams
            id. 9.031
            b. 17.07.1958 Melbourne, Vic
            m. 30.11.2010 Box Hill, Vic

            Cheng Xiao Hue
            id. 9.031A
            b. 15.11.1963 Qinghai, China

            Cheng Longyi
            id. 10.043 (Stepson to Michael)
            b. 08.09.1988 Shaanxi, China

        Cullen Hamlet Budd
        id. 8.018
        b. 1930
        d. 1931 Warragul, Vic

        Earl Lewin Budd
        id. 8.021
        b. 1932 Traralgon. Vic
        d. 1932 Traralgon. Vic

        Silver Merle Lilian Margaret Budd
        id. 8.023
        b. 23.04.1934 Allambee, Vic
        m. 03.10.1953 East Melbourne, Vic

        Brian Daniel Burgess
        id. 8.023A
        b. 09.04.1928 Echuca, Vic

        m.dd.mm.1987
        d. 28.10.2009, b'd Echuca, Vic

        Keith Mc Fadden
        id. 8.023B

            Robert John Burgess
            id. 9.026
            h. 06.08.1956 Sunshine. Vic
            m.06.06.1981 Echuca, Vic

            Kaye Lynette Saddlier
            id. 9.026A
            b. 14.10.1959 Cohuna. Vic

                 Ryan Daniel Burgess
                id. 10.031
                b. 12.11.1984 Echuca, Vic

                Logan John Burgess
                id. 10.035
                b. 09.09.1986 Echuca, Vic

Peter Anthony Burgess
id. 9.030
b. 14.06.1958 Pearcedale, Vic
m. 26.01.1980 Echuca, Vic

m.

m.10.06.2006 Pakenham, Vic

Deborah May Peatling
id. 9.030A
b. 14.12.1961 Kerang, Vic

Glenda Hutchinson
id. 9.030B

Stephanie Urbancic
id. 9.030C
b. 18.12.1953 Slovenia

Gavin James Burgess
id. 9.035
b. 08.03.1960 Frankston, Vic
m.28.04.1990 Echuca, Vic

Joanne Margaret Honey
id. 9.035A
b. 14.11.1965 Echuca, Vic

    Brooke Veronica Burgess
    id. 10.048
    b. 26.07.1989 Echuca, Vic

    Reece Desmond Burgess
    id. 10.062
    b. 02.07.1991 Echuca, Vic

    Jake James Burgess
    id. 10.076
    b. 26.09.1993 Echuca, Vic

Karen Lynette Burgess
id. 9.083 Adopted
b.11.07.1972 Melbourne, Vic
m. 03.05.2003 Kyabram, Vic

Darren Ross Glasson
id. 9.083A
b. 07.11.1969 Rochester, Vic

    Natasha Zoe Glasson
    id. 10.104
    b. 18.01.1999 Kyabram, Vic

    Victoria Rose Glasson
    id. 10.151
    b. 30.06.2009 Kyabram, Vic

Brenda Elaine Budd
id. 8.030
b. 18.02.1936 Trafalgar, Vic
m. 22.12.1956 Brighton, Vic
d. 16.02.2011 Box Hill, Vic

Clarence Norman Kneebone
id. 8.030A
b. 03.06.1933 Wangaratta, Vic
d. 08.04.2012 Belgrave, Vic

Peter Norman Kneebone
id. 9.029
b. 11.01.1958 Melbourne, Vic
m. 16.05.1981 Brighton, Vic

Nicolette Dixon
id. 9.029A
b. 22.02.1960 Ballarat, Vic

    Matthew Norman Kneebone
    id.10.022
    b. 06.10.1981 Ferntree Gully, Vic

    Kristy Peta Kneebone
    id.10.027
    b. 14.02.1984 Ferntree Gully, Vic

        Kayden Kneebone
        id. 11.013
        b. 2005

        James Kneebone
        id.11.024
        b. 2011

Stephen Leslie Kneebone
id. 9.041
b. 18.05.1961 Melbourne, Vic
m.10.01.1980 Ferntree Gully, Vic

Diane Raylene Finch
id. 9.041A
b. 07.01.1963 Morwell, Vic

    Tracey Lee Kneebone
    id. 10.023
    b. 22.11.1981 Ferntree Gully, Vic

    Geoffrey Ian Delphin
    id. 10.023A
    b. 25.03.1975 Pakenham, Vic

    Dylan Tristan Delphin
    id. 11.008
    b. 07.05.2002 Traralgon, Vic

    Caitlyn Louise Kneebone
    id. 11.012
    b. 16.11.2004 Traralgon, Vic

m. 16.11.1985 Kallista, Vic

    Sharon Leigh O'Neill
    id. 9.041B
    b. 12.12.1963 Ringwood, Vic

Tamara Jade Kneebone
id. 10.036
b. 18.11.1986 Ferntree Gully, Vic

Daniel Nathan Kneebone
id. 10.050
b. 13.09.1989 Cobram, Vic

Shannon Rebecca Kneebone
id. 10.070
b. 24.09.1992 Melbourne, Vic

Joshua David Kneebone
id. 10.088
b. 26.10.1995 Finley, NSW

Cheryl Elaine Kneebone
id. 9.059
b. 23.05.1966 Box Hill, Vic
m.06.05.1989 Kallista, Vic

Christopher Callaghan
id. 9.059A
b. 24.06.1963 Halifax, England

Jessica Rose Callaghan
id. 10.049
b. 08.09.1989 Ferntree Gully, Vic

Scott Christopher Myles Callaghan
id. 10.060
b. 20.05.1991 Ferntree Gully, Vic

Jackson Leigh Callaghan
id. 10.084
b. 28.04.1995 Ferntree Gully, Vic

Nelson Clarence Budd
id. 8.035
b. 01.06.1938 Trafalgar, Vic
d. 18.05.1964 Ararat, Vic

Clarence Thomas Rbt Wm Henderson
id. 7.024
b. 25.06.1898 Curlewis, Vic
m.28.12.1932 Childers, Vic
d. 16.07.1983 b'd Fawkner, Vic

Iris Elsie Berry
id. 7.024A
b. 06.08.1914 Ulverstone, Tas
d. 09.01.1979 b'd Fawkner, Vic

Clarence Henderson
id. 8.022
b. 11.11.1933 Trafalgar, Vic
d.13.11.1933 b'd Trafalgar, Vic

Margaret Jessie Iris Henderson
id. 8.029
b. 10.05.1936 Trafalgar, Vic
m. 14.05.1955 Brunswick, Vic

Ronald Leslie Atkinson
id. 8.029A
b.23.08.1933 Carlton, Vic

Wayne Edward Atkinson
id. 9.024
b. 11.02.1956 Carlton, Vic
m. 17.01.1993 Darnum, Vic

Anne Marie McNiffe
id. 9.024A
b. 31.01.1958 Yallourn, Vic

Clare Rose Atkinson
id. 10.093
b. 29.08.1996 Warragul, Vic

Gail Christine Atkinson
id. 9.028
b. 12.10.1957 Carlton, Vic
m. 23.01.1978 St Kilda, Vic

David Brian Higgins
id. 9.028A
b. 31.08.1956 McKinnon, Vic

Leonard John Higgins
id. 10.061
b. 25.05.1991 Bendigo, Vic

Gareth Leslie Higgins
id. 10.073
b. 09.05.1993 Warrnambool, Vic

Rodney William Atkinson
id. 9.032
b. 28.11.1958 Carlton, Vic
m. 11.02.1985 Moe, Vic

Yvonne Dezaayer
id. 9.032A
b.09.03.1961 Yallourn, Vic

Karen Hartrick
id. 9.032B
b. 27.01.1952 Mentone, Vic

Zoe Grace Atkinson
id. 10.058
b. 08.02.1991 Warragul, Vic

Samuel William Atkinson
id. 10.068
b. 04.09.1992 Warragul, Vic

Brian Ronald Atkinson
id. 9.036
b. 21.03.1960 Carlton, Vic
m. 01.08.1981 Newborough, Vic

Beverley Anne Richards
id. 9.036A
b.10.12.1962 Yallourn, Vic

    Bianca Patricia Atkinson
    id. 10.024
    b. 04.12.1981 Moe, Vic

    Daniel Jay McNamara
    id. 10.024A

        Courtnie Amber McNamara
        id. 11.009
        b. 05.03.2003 Traralgon, Vic

        Zoe Jade McNamara
        id. 11.011
        b. 15.02.2004 Traralgon, Vic

    m. 16.10.2010 Moe, Vic

    Heath Richard Stray
    id. 10.024B
    b. 28.08.1987 Moe, Vic

    Brooke Kira Atkinson
    id. 10.028
    b. 31.05.1984 Moe, Vic

    Russell John Chessum
    id. 10.028A
    b. 19.08.1979 Morwell, Vic

        Chelsea Anne Chessum
        id. 11.021
        b. 14.04.2010 Traralgon, Vic

    Bradley Raymond Atkinson
    id. 10.034
    b. 31.01.1986 Moe, Vic

Gavin Raymond Atkinson
id. 9.045
b. 18.06.1962 Carlton, Vic

Donna Casey
id. 9.045A
b. 03.05.1965 Berwick, Vic

    Daniel James Atkinson
    id. 10.052
    b. 21.10.1989 Moe, Vic

    Olivia Nicole Atkinson
    id. 10.063
    b. 26.07.1991 Moe, Vic

    Jodie Lee Atkinson
    id. 10.095
    b. 07.11.1996 Moe, Vic

Jennifer Robyn Atkinson
id. 9.049
b. 20.08.1963 Carlton, Vic
m. 08.11.1986 Moe, Vic

Garry John Jacobs
id. 9.049A
b. 30.09.1961 Mirboo North, Vic

    Brylie Leah Jacobs
    id. 10.040
    b. 22.12.1987 Moe, Vic

    Teoni Ellen Jacobs
    id. 10.047
    b. 12.07.1989 Moe, Vic

    Rhys Dylan Jacobs
    id. 10.067
    b. 17.01.1992 Moe, Vic

Janine Susan Atkinson
id. 9.054
b. 16.02.1965 Preston, Vic
m. 24.01.1987 Trafalgar, Vic

Jackson Long
id. 9.054A
b. 09.10.1959 Yallourn, Vic

    Thomas Ryan Long
    id. 10.038
    b. 07.11.1987 Moe, Vic

    Jarrod Tyler Long
    id. 10.051
    b. 17.09.1989 Moe, Vic

    Darcy Jackson Long
    id. 10.064
    b. 08.08.1991 Moe, Vic

    Dylan Brodie Long
    id. 10.074
    b. 11.05.1993 Moe, Vic

Lucy Henderson
id. 8.033
b. xx.04.1938 Trafalgar, Vic
d. xx.04.1938 Trafalgar, Vic

Brian Clarence Henderson   **Joan Wilma Matthews**
id. 8.043   id. 8.043A
b. 18.06.1943 Carlton, Vic   b. 11.04.1940
m. 05.10.1963 Reservoir, Vic

    Paul William Henderson   **Cheryl Anne Blewitt**
    id. 9.055   id. 9.055A
    b. 09.03.1965 Richmond, Vic   b. circa 1969
    m. 1991 Urana, NSW

        David Henderson
        id. 10.044
        b. 04.10.1988 Preston, Vic

        Blake Henderson
        id. 10.065
        b. 11.10.1991 Albury, NSW

        Kurt Henderson
        id. 10.086
        b. 20.09.1995 Preston, Vic

    Joanne Henderson   **Trevor McLean**
    id. 9.063   id.9.063A
    b. 25.01.1967 Reservoir, Vic

        Jessie McLean
        id.10.046
        b. 11.07.1989 Preston, Vic

        Reece McLean
        id. 10.071
        b. 17.11.1992 Ballina, NSW

    Craig Brian Henderson
    id. 9.101
    b. 16.05.1976 Reservoir, Vic

Nelson James Albert Henderson
id. 7.030
b. 21.10.1905 Mirboo North, Vic
d. 16.01.1909 b'd Yarragon, Vic

Alberta Margaret Victoria Henderson   **Eric Fowler**
id. 7.038   id. 7.038A
b. 21.04.1916 Warragul, Vic
m. circa 1942

m. circa 1960   **Frank Henderson**
                                                                     id. 7.038B

m.xx. 09.1965 Melbourne, Vic   **Wattie Chuck**
d. xx. 08.1966 b'd Mirboo North, Vic   id. 7.038C
                                                                     d. circa 1966

APPENDIX 20

WILLIAM THOM OF AUSTRALIA

William Nathaniel Walter Hamlet Thom
id. 6.028
b. 11.12.1881 St Leonards Vic
m. 17.05.1905 Geelong, Vic

m. 1948 Geelong, Vic
d. 21.06.1957 b'd Geelong West, Vic

Lilian Potter
id. 6.028A
b.1883 Geelong, Vic
d. 22.08.1947 b'd Geelong West, Vic

Lucinda Pike (nee Larty)
id. 6.028B
b. 1883
d. b'd 22.7.1953 Fawkner, Vic

  Gladys Lilian Thom
  id. 7.032
  b. xx.04.1906 Yarragon, Vic
  d. 16.01.1910 b'd Geelong West, Vic

  Geoffrey Walter Thom
  id. 7.034
  b. 28.04.1910 Geelong, Vic
  m. 13.04.1935 Geelong, Vic
  d. 16.03.1973 b'd Geelong West, Vic

  Doris May Cortous
  id. 7.034A
  b. 20.11.1912 Geelong, Vic
  d. 14.08.2008 b'd Geelong West, Vic

    Brian Geoffrey Thom
    id. 8.028
    b. 24.02.1936 Geelong, Vic
    m. 13.02.1960 Geelong, Vic.

    m.08.10.1993 Geelong, Vic

    Jillienne Rae Hookings
    id. 8.028A
    b. 28.04.1936 Mt Gambier, SA

    Elwyn Joy Roberts (nee Russell)
    id. 8.028B
    b. 16.12.1937 Geelong, Vic

      Sally Elizabeth Thom
      id. 9.043
      b. 18.08.1961 Geelong, Vic

      Raymond Reginald Holt Row
      id. 9.043A
      b. 07.10.1957 Bundaberg, Qld

        Lucy Elizabeth Thom
        id. 10.072
        b. 15.04.1993 Geelong, Vic

      Susan Louise Thom
      id. 9.050
      b. 10.10.1963 Geelong, Vic
      m. 05.10.2003 Geelong, Vic

      Frederick Alexander Horne
      id. 9.050A
      b. 29.09.1948 Carlton, Vic

      Catherine Jean Thom
      id. 9.057
      b. 04.11.1965 Geelong, Vic
      m. 16.04.1994 Geelong, Vic

      Peter Craig Schwarz
      id. 9.057A
      b. 10.12.1968 Geelong, Vic

        Benjamin Robert Schwarz
        id. 10.081
        b. 02.10.1994 Geelong, Vic

        Emily Jean Schwarz
        id. 10.097
        b. 30.04.1997 Geelong, Vic

        Adam James Schwarz
        id. 10.114
        b. 12.06.2001 Geelong, Vic

      Lisa Jane Thom
      id. 9.072
      b. 12.12.1970 Geelong, Vic
      m. 14.04.1996 Geelong, Vic

      Colin James Marshall
      id. 9.072A
      b. 06.02.1970 Geelong, Vic

        Ruby Jean Marshall
        id. 10.111
        b. 12.11.2000 Melbourne, Vic

        Thomas James Marshall
        id. 10.112
        b. 12.11.2000 Melbourne, Vic
        d. 17.11.2000 b'd Geelong West, Vic

        Oliver James Marshall
        id. 10.128
        b. 31.08.2004 Geelong, Vic

Noel Lindsay Thom
id. 8.038
b. 24.09.1940 Geelong, Vic
m. 07.01.1966 Hamilton, Vic

Patricia Ann Rankin
id. 8.038A
b. 08.11.1942 Hamilton, Vic

    Megan Joanne Thom
    id. 9.078
    b. 04.02.1972 Geelong, Vic
    m. 09.02.2002 Geelong Vic

    Justin Andrew Goodes
    id.9.078A
    b. 16.12.1970 Ringwood, Vic

    Sarah Kristen Thom
    id. 9.091
    b. 16.03.1974 Geelong, Vic

Carolyn Faye Thom
id. 8.047
b. 06.05.1945 Geelong, Vic
m. 20.12.1967 Geelong, Vic

John Desmond Harvey
id. 8.047A
b. 08.08.1932 Camperdown, Vic
d. 15.01.1997 b'd Melbourne, Vic

m. 20.10.2000 Hampton, Vic

Paul de Smit
id. 8.047B
b. 15.04.1943 Amsterdam, Netherlands

    Jodie Danielle Harvey
    id. 9.082 adopted
    b. 30.04.1972 Geelong, Vic
    m. 18.03.2006 Cairns, Qld

    Jeffrey Joseph Williams
    id. 9.082A
    b. 27.08.1960 North Ryde, NSW

        Jack Desmond Williams
        id.10.141
        b. 20.02.2007 Plymouth, England

    Christopher Geoffrey Harvey
    id. 9.089
    b. 13.12.1973 Melbourne, Vic
    m. 11.01.2004 Mt Eliza, Vic

    Caroline Audrey Johnson
    id. 9.089A
    b. 07.07.1977 Melbourne, Vic

        Charlee Mae Harvey
        id. 10.127
        b. 29.08.2004 Melbourne, Vic

        Lila Anais Harvey
        id. 10.143
        b. 30.10.2007 Melbourne, Vic

Albert Edward Thom
id. 7.036
b. 30.09.1911 Thorpdale, Vic
m. 02.05.1936 Bendigo, Vic
d. 02.11.1984. b'd Geelong West, Vic

Beryl May Cravino
id. 7.036A
b. 23.06.1917 Bendigo, Vic
d. 16.02.2012 b'd Geelong West Vic

    Graeme Edward Thom
    id. 8.032
    b. 16.01.1938 Geelong, Vic
    d. 08.02.1951. b'd Geelong West, Vic

    Colin William Thom
    id. 8.037
    b. 19.05.1940 Geelong, Vic
    m.10.03.1967 Ballarat, Vic

    Shirley Anne Crothall
    id. 8.037A
    b. 16.09.1943 London, England

    Fraser Colin McGregor Thom
    id. 9.070
    b. 09.05.1970 Geelong, Vic
    m.06.10.2012 Melbourne, Vic

    Vanessa Jane West
    id. 9.070A
    b. 23.07.1975 Melbourne Vic

    Melinda Elizabeth Thom
    id. 9.077
    b. 14.11.1971 Geelong, Vic
    m. 01.10.1994 Noosa, Qld

    Steven John Hughes
    id. 9.077A
    b. 16.06.1964 London, England

        William John Hughes
        id. 10.098
        b. 19.09.1997 Redcliffe, Qld

        Winston Thom Raymond Hughes
        id.10.109
        b. 13.09.2000 Redcliffe, Qld

Darryl Ernest Thom
id. 8.039
b. 23.04.1942 Bendigo, Vic
m. 01.12.1966 Geelong, Vic
d. 30.09.2008 Brisbane, Qld

Maureen McLean
id. 8.039A
b. 17.01.1944 Geelong, Vic
d. 26.03.2004 Brisbane, Qld

Susan Louise Thom
id. 9.085
b. 20.10.1972 Brisbane, Qld
m.14.10.1995 Brisbane, Qld

m. 15.07.2004 Hong Kong

Julian Marcus Sheezel
id. 9.085A
b. 30.01.1970 Melbourne, Vic

Christopher Stuart Blair
id. 9.085B
b. 26.02.1964 Port Moresby, PNG

Jordan Sebastian James Blair
id. 10.078 Stepson to Susan
b. 07.12. 1993 Hong Kong

Niall Ambrose Blair
id 10.085 Stepson to Susan
b. 18.08.1995 Hong Kong

Maxwell Thomson Blair
id. 10.131
b. 19.05.2005 Hong Kong

Grace May Blair
id. 10.157
b. 22.04.2012 Doha, Qatar

APPENDIX 21

MABEL HIND OF AUSTRALIA

Mabel Beatrice Louisa Jane Thom
id. 6.029
b. 08.05.1885 St Leonards Vic
m.12.08.1903 Melbourne, Vic
d. 22.03.1970 Dromana, Vic

James Henry Claridge Hind
id. 6.029A
b. 06.06.1879 Warnambool, Vic
d. 10.09.1948 b'd Fawkner, Vic

    Alexander Joseph James Hind
    id. 7.029
    b. 21.05.1905 Jumbunna, NSW
    m. 1932 Victoria

    m. 16.05.1974
    d. 23.10.1985 Penrith, NSW

    Vera Edith Cook
    id. 7.029A
    d.1973

    Phyllis Anne Hall
    id. 7.029B
    b. 10.04.1909 Ringwood, Vic

        Neville Alexander Hind
        id. 8.024
        b. circa 1934
        m. circa 1970
        d. 06.01.1976 b'd Springvale, Vic

        Denise Eleanor Reynolds
        id. 8.024A

    Isabel Mabel Elizabeth Hind
    id. 7.033
    b. 18.01.1907 Yarra Glen, Vic
    m. 1931 Victoria
    d. 15.05.1971 b'd Fawkner, Vic

    George Crawford Knight
    id. 7.033A
    b. circa 1890 Scotland
    d 1961 Heidelberg, Vic

        Colin Alexander Robert Knight
        id. 8.019
        b. 02.08.1931 Carlton, Vic
        m.
        d.2007 b'd Fawkner, Vic

        Muriel Sylvia Cameron
        id. 8.019A
        b. 15.03.1927

            Peter Anthony Knight
            id.9.053
            b. 22.11.1964

Robert Claridge Hind
id. 7.035
b. 26.01.1911 Hastings, Vic
m. 1933 Victoria
d. 29.11.1976 b'd Lilydale, Vic

Ivy May Kingsland
id. 7.035A
b. 13.02.1910
d. 11.09.1972 b'd Lilydale, Vic

    Robert Claridge Hind
    id. 8.025
    b. 18.09.1934 Fawkner, Vic
    m. 20.10.1952 Melbourne, Vic
    d. 03.06.1983 Creswick, Vic

    Kathleen Patricia Overmars
    id. 8.025A
    b. 11.09.1935 Clifton Hill, Vic

        Cheryl Robin Hind
        id. 9.020
        b. 25.03.1954 Hampton, Vic
        m. 06.03.1971 Glenroy, Vic

        Stephen Campion
        id. 9.020A
        b. 19.02.1949 Lancaster, England

            Michelle Anne Campion
            id. 10.004
            b. 10.09.1971 Glenroy, Vic

            John Francis Ware
            id. 10.004A
            b. 01.04.1974

                Jacob Francis Ware
                id. 11.001
                b. 31.08.1995

                Brenton James Ware
                id. 11.002
                b. 16.06.1998

            Debbie Jane Campion
            id. 10.013
            b. 26.00.1077 Glenroy, Vic
            m.

            Glenn Douglas Maguire
            id. 10.013A
            b.24.02.1077

Hannah Jane Maguire
id. 11.004
b. 27.12.2000

Fletcher Glenn Maguire
id. 11.007
b.10.01.2003

Jude Stephen Maguire
id. 11.010
b.14.08.2004

Janice Gay Hind
id. 9.023
b. 14.01.1956 Mansfield, Vic
m. 22.05.1977 Clunes, Vic

Gregory Bruce Allen
id. 9.023A
b. 21.08.1953 Ararat, Vic

Donna Joan Allen
id. 10.012
b. 05.05.1977 Clunes, Vic

Jennifer Isobel Allen
id. 10.016
b. 29.01.1979 Clunes, Vic

Robbie James Allen
id. 10.021
b. 30.05.1981 Clunes, Vic

Catherine Annette Hind
id. 9.027
b. 05.09.1957 Richmond, Vic
m. 16.02.1974 Ballarat, Vic

Eric George Allen
id. 9.027A
b. 13.12 1955 Ararat, Vic

Mark Stephen Allen
id. 10.008
b. 30.07.1974 Ballarat, Vic

Bree Louise McCormack
id. 10.008A
b. 25.07.1984

Summer Annette Allen
id. 11.018
b. 04.01.2009

Ayva Bree Allen
id. 11.020
b. 19.02.2010

Michael John Allen
id. 10.018
b. 17.06.1980 Ballarat, Vic
m. 14.11.2008

Sarah Elaynah McKenzie
id. 10.018A
b. 05.08.1985

Xenia Elaynah Allen
id.11.014
b. 08.12.2005

Axel Pockets Allen
id.11.019
b. 22.08.2009

m.10.06.1989 Ballarat, Vic

Neville James Richards
id. 9.027B
b. 30.04.1964 Ballarat, Vic

Caitlin Elouise Richards
id. 10.055
b. 04.05.1990 Ballarat, Vic

Patrick Charles Richards
id. 10.077
b. 04.11.1993 Creswick, Vic

Robert William Hind
id. 9.034
b. 05.02.1960 Richmond, Vic
m. 07.11.1981 Ballarat, Vic

Louise Maria Rieniets
id. 9.034A
b. 01.03.1961 Clunes, Vic

Robert Terence Hind
id. 10.033
b. 10.04.1985 Clunes, Vic

Greer Louise Hind
id. 10.037
b. 06.01.1987 Ballarat, Vic
d. 06.01.1987 b'd Clunes, Vic

Lee Stephen Hind
id. 10.042
b. 06.04.1988 Ballarat, Vic

Peter Thomas Hind
id. 10.053
b. 14.12.1989 Ballarat, Vic

Raymond James Hind   **Susan Louise Wade**
id. 9.040   id. 9.040A
b. 26.02.1961 Richmond, Vic   b. 19.04.1962 Melbourne, Vic

James Wade Hind
id.10.041
b. 12.01.1988 Ballarat, Vic

Matthew Dean Hind   **Ashlee Maree Bahl**
id.10.045   id. 10.045A
b. 11.11.1988 Ballarat, Vic   b. 22.06.1988 Ballarat, Vic

Kaiden Matthew Hind
id. 11.022
b. 01.09.2010 Ballarat, Vic

John Charles Hind   **Rebecca XXX**
id. 9.064   id. 9.064A
b. 16.07.1967 Glenroy, Vic

Jayden Hind
id. 10.054
b, 1990?

Nicholas Hind
id. 10.066
b. 1992?

Lachlan Hind
id. 10.080
b.1994?

Emilee Hind
id. 10.090
b. 1996?

Valerie June Hind   **Brian Mc Kie**
id. 8.026   id. 8.026
b. 09.03.1935 Melbourne, Vic   b. 23.12.1934 Melbourne, Vic
m. 09.03.1955 Melbourne, Vic

Gayle Patricia McKie   **Kurt Kuffer**
id. 9.025   id. 9.025A
b. 22.05.1956 Melbourne, Vic   b. 07.07.1954 Switzerland
m. 28.08.1974 Lilydale, Vic

Michelle Deanne Kuffer
id. 10.011
b. 21.06.1975 Liverpool, NSW

Aaron Jason Kuffer
id. 10.014
b. 06.01.1978 Rosebud, Vic

Kerryn Ann Mc Kie   **Brian Pearce**
id. 9.037   id. 9.037A
b. 11.06.1960 Melbourne, Vic   b. 21.04.1959 Islington, England
m. 22.03.1980 Mt Dandenong, Vic

Ashlea June Pearce
id. 10.039
b. 10.11.1987 Ballarat, Vic

Susan Dea Mc Kie
id. 9.065
b. 27.10.1967 Melbourne, Vic

James Henry Hind
id. 8.031
b. 23.10.1937 Fawkner, Vic
m. 02.06.1962 Croydon, Vic

Christine Humphrey
id. 8.031
b. 26.08.1943 Maryborough, Vic
d. 25.05.2008

   David James Hind
   id. 9.047
   b. 11.04.1963 Boxhill, Vic
   m. 12.09.1987 Croydon, Vic

   Marnie Elizabeth Clutton
   id. 9.047A
   b. 14.12.1964 Surrey, England

      Peter James Hind
      id. 10.057
      b. 27.01.1991 Lilydale, Vic

      Cassandra Elizabeth Hind
      id. 10.069
      b. 04.09.1992 Lilydale, Vic

      Sarah Louise Hind
      id. 10.083
      b. 08.04.1995 Mansfield, Vic

   Mark Henry Hind
   id. 9.061
   b. 19.08.1966 Melbourne, Vic

   Jamie Robert Hind
   id. 9.069
   b. 11.03.1969 Lilydale, Vic
   m.

   Leonie Strachan
   id. 9.069A

      Rebecca Hind
      id.10.091
      b. 07.03. 1996

      Aaron Hind
      id. 10.101
      b. 24.07.1998

      Justin Hind
      id. 10.115
      b. 26.10.2001

      Stacey Hind
      id. 10.117
      b. 24.02.2003

   Kelly Anne Hind
   id. 9.093
   b. 27.08.1974 Lilydale, Vic

   XXXX Estcourt
   id. 9.093A

      Stephanie Nicole Estcourt
      id. 10.075
      b. 21.09.1993 Lilydale, Vic

      Jayde Amy Estcourt
      id. 10.094
      b. 06.09.1996 Lilydale, Vic

   Christopher Leigh Studley
   id. 9.093B
   b. 15.08.1969 Bendigo, Vic

      Jordyn Leigh Studley
      id.10.108
      b. 31.07.2000 Box Hill, Vic

      Brianna Jane Studley
      id. 10.120
      b. 03.06.2003 Box Hill, Vic

Pamela Gay Hind
id. 8.044
b. 08.12.1944
m. 06.01.1962 Mooralbark, Vic

Joseph Matthew Bemelmans
id. 8.044A
b. 08.04.1942

   Julie Mae Bemelmans
   id. 9.048
   b. 11.07.1963
   m. 23.10.1983 Mooralbark, Vic

   Gregory Peter Carrigan
   id. 9.048A
   b. 29.05.1960
   d. 24.03.2009 Canberra, ACT

Davis Matthew Carrigan
id. 10.029
b. 20.06.1984

Steven Matthew Bemelmans
id. 9.060
b. 30.07.1966

Leesa Ann Bemelmans
id. 9.081
b. 25.04.1972

Eva Victoria Dillon Hind
id. 7.037
b. 08.08.1915 Sth Melbourne, Vic
m.14.11.1936 Trawool, Vic
d. 17.05.1995

Henry Albert Alexander Powell
id. 7.037A
b. 13.11.1910 London, England

James Henry Powell
id. 8.034
b. 20.05.1938 Carlton, Vic
m.24.03.1962 Sandringham, Vic

m.12.07.1980 Rowville, Vic

Norma Anne Schukraft
id. 8.034A
b. 12.05.1940 Sandringham, Vic

Pamela Coutts
id. 8.034B

Bronwyn Denise Powell
id. 9.068
b. 08.11.1968 Springvale, Vic

Geoffrey James Powell
id. 9.074
b. 04.03.1971 Springvale, Vic

Henry Powell
id. 8.041
b. 30.09.1942 Carlton, Vic
m.19.06.1965 Highett, Vic

Lorraine Terry
id. 8.041A
b. 05.11.1944 Dapto, NSW

Carl Henry Powell
id. 9.058
b. 19.12.1965 Sandringham,Vic

Micah James Powell
id. 9.067
b. 06.06.1968 Chelsea, Vic

Katherine Louise Powell
id. 9.071
b. 13.05.1970 Mordialloc, Vic
d. 19.06.1971

Anthony John Powell
id. 9.087
b. 28.07.1973 Chelsea, Vic

Stephen David Powell
id. 9.113
b. 20.05.1983

Alan Powell
id. 8.049
b. 11.09.1946

Robert Powell
id. 8.054
b. 25.02.1950
m. 20.11.1971 Belgrave, Vic

Joan Ellen Pike
id. 8.054A
b. 03.10.1949

Narelle Louise Powell
id. 9.092
b. 14.08.1974 Frankston, Vic

Shane Robert Powell
id. 9.103
b. 11.03.1977 Frankston, Vic

James Thomas Hind
id. 7.039
b. 30.07.1917 North Melbourne, Vic
m.06.01.1945 Brunswick, Vic
d. 04.09.1972 b'd Broadford, Vic

Jessie Elizabeth Goff
id. 7.039A
b. 08.02.1924 Coburg, Vic
d. 04.03.2010 b'd Broadford, Vic

   Carol Anne Hind
   id. 8.051
   b. 27.09.1947 Melbourne, Vic
   m.23.12.1962 Coburg, Vic

   Kenneth Mervyn McKenzie
   id. 8.051A
   b. 15.05.1938 Canterbury, Vic

      Karen Lynda McKenzie
      id. 9.066
      b. 03.04.1968 Yea, Vic

Norman James William Hind
id. 8.055
b. 27.09.1950 Broadford, Vic
m.11.03.1972 Heidelberg, Vic

Carol Anne Langley
id. 8.055A
b. 26.09.1958 Ivanhoe, Vic

   Leslie James Hind
   id. 9.097
   b. 08.11.1975 Albury, NSW
   m.04.11.2000 Melbourne, Vic

   Michelle Louise Zytek
   id. 9.097A
   b. 26.09.1975 Greensborough, Vic

      Aaron Helmut Hind
      id. 10.087
      b. 20.10.1995 Preston. Vic

      Hayden Mark Hind
      id.10.099
      b. 26.09.1997 Preston, Vic

      Jamie Christopher Hind
      id. 10.107
      b. 16.03.2000 Preston, Vic

      Jessica Elizabeth Hind
      id. 10.118
      b. 13.03.2003 Epping, Vic

      Emily Veronica Hind
      id. 10.129
      b. 01.02.2005 Epping, Vic
      d. 01.02.2005 b'd Seymour, Vic

      Zachary James Hind
      id. 10.137
      b. 09.01.2006 Heidelberg, Vic

      Riley William Hind
      id.10.149
      b. 10.03.2009 Heidelberg, Vic

   Michelle Anne Hind
   id. 9.107
   b. 19.09.1978 Kilmore, Vic

   m.

   Margaret Mary Abela
   id. 8.055B
   b. 23.04.1962 Malta

John Henry Hind
id. 8.057
b. 29.01.1952 Broadford, Vic
m. circa 1972

Kerri Elizabeth Tobin
id. 8.057A
b. 02.04.1957 Ballarat, Vic

   Tracey Lee Hind
   id. 9.084
   b. 08.08.1972 Seymour, Vic
   m.28.12.1995 Olinda, Vic

   Mark Tracy Clarisse
   id. 9.084
   b. 10.06.1971 Richmond, Vic

      Bailey Jacob Clarisse
      id.10.103
      b. 20.09.1998 Noble Park, Vic

      Holly Rose Clarisse
      id. 10.113
      b. 05.06.2001 Dandenong, Vic

Rubie Mae Clarisse
id. 10.122
b. 06.11.2003 Upper Fern Tree Gully, Vic

Matthew John Hind
id. 9.099
b. 26.01.1976 Mildura, Vic
d. 16.10.1982 Drouin, Vic

Colin Joseph Claridge Hind   **Karen Meggs**
id. 8.059   id. 8.059A
b. 10.10.1955 Broadford, Vic
m.

Heath Andrew Hind
id. 9.111
b. 04.07.1982 Fitzroy, Vic

m. dd.05.1986 Kilmore, Vic   **June Hanson**
                                             id. 8.059B
                                             b. 18.07.1946 Heathcote, Vic

Bessie Mabel Kathleen Hind   **Richard Frederick Plastow**
id. 7.041   id. 7.041A
b. 19.01.1922 South Melbourne, Vic   b. 06.01.1919 Chiltern, Vic
m.13.03.1943 Coburg, Vic   d. 18.04.1988 b'd Numurkah, Vic
d. 02.06.2007 b'd Numurkah, Vic

Lorraine Joy Plastow   **David George Turbett**
id. 8.046   id. 8.046A
b. 21.03.1945 East Coburg, Vic   b. 22.04.1948 Perth, WA
m.17.10.1970 Perth, WA

Paul Steven Turbett   **Joanne Karen Logan**
id. 9.075   id. 9.075A
b. 04.04.1971 Perth, WA   b. 31.07.1971 Adelaide, SA
m.17.02.2007 Perth, WA

Glenda Karen Turbett   **Michael David Bundle**
id. 9.088   id. 9.088A
b. 05.08.1973 West Coburg, Vic   b. 25.08.1965 London, England
m. 25.10.2003 Perth, WA   d. 25.10.2006 Palmers Green, London

m. 04.04.2010 Caversham, WA   **Craig Robert Adams**
                                             id. 9.088B
                                             b.24.09.1969 Perth, WA

Sophie Mae Adams
id. 10.155
b. 13.11.2011 Perth, WA

Beverley Joy Plastow   **Kevin John Wain**
id. 8.048   id. 8.048A
b. 06.05.1946 East Coburg, Vic   b. 19.12.1938 Chiltern, Vic
m.16.05.1970 Coburg, Vic   d. 30.08.1999 b'd Numurkah, Vic

David Kevin Wain   **Belinda Jane Chisholm**
id. 9.073   id. 9.073A
b. 20.02.1971 Numurkah, Vic   b. 04.09.1973 Melbourne, Vic
m.18.03.2000 Kew, Vic

Brayden Kevin Wain
id. 10.119
b. 29.03.2003 Bundoora, Vic

Lachlan Flynn Wain
id. 10.139
b. 06.12.2006 Bundoora, Vic

Cooper Richard Wain
id. 10.154
b. 27.02.2011 Heidelberg, Vic

Julie Joy Wain   **Michael James Buha**
id. 9.079   id. 9.079A
b. 16.02.1972 Numurkah, Vic   b. 06.01.1970 Shepparton, Vic
m.07.03.1998 Numurkah, Vic

Nathan Josip Buha
id. 10.121
b. 10.08.2003 Shepparton, Vic
d. 23.03.2004 b'd Numurkah, Vic

Kate Natalie Buha
id. 10.132
b. 10.08.2005 Shepparton, Vic

Luke Nathan Buha
id. 10.144
b. 31.10.2007 Shepparton, Vic

Edwin James Plastow
id. 8.053
b. 07.01.1950 East Coburg, Vic
m.23.02.1974 Pascoe Vale, Vic

Pauline Margaret Awty
id. 8.053A
b. 29.07.1953 Melbourne, Vic
d. 08.09.2004 Epping, Vic

Sally Elizabeth Plastow
id. 9.104
b. 24.06.1977 Chelsea, Vic
m.11.01.2003 Melbourne, Vic

Adam John Friend
id. 9.104A
b. 10.08.1976 Moonee Ponds, Vic

Angus James William Friend
id. 10.148
b. 16.10.2008 Heidelberg, Vic

Oliver Alexander Elgar Friend
id. 10.152
b. 22.01.2010 Heidelberg, Vic

m. 19.01.1985 Reservoir, Vic

Valerie McDonald
id. 8.053B
b.10.05.1953 Melbourne, Vic

Zoe Margaret Plastow
id. 9.115
b. 28.12.1989 Benalla, Vic

Mabel Marjory Hind
id. 7.042
b. 18.12.1927 Brunswick, Vic
m.18.12.1948 Coburg, Vic

William James Pratt
id. 7.042A
b. 15.05.1926 Richmond, Vic

Christine Janice Pratt
id. 8.056
b. 06.04.1951 Coburg, Vic
m.12.05.1973 Southport, Qld

Kelvin Wiremu Fisher
id. 8.056A
b. 31.03.1949 Riverton, NZ

Melissa Jane Eriti Fisher
id. 9.095
b. 27.05.1975 Mornington, Vic
m.08.11.2003 Mornington, Vic

Andrew Carl Pemberton
id. 9.095A
b. 16.07.1981 Frankston, Vic

Maurice Andrew Werimu Pemberton
id. 10.134
b. 17.09.2005 Frankston, Vic

Thomas Tamuera Pemberton
id. 10.146
b. 08.04.2008 Frankston, Vic

Michelle Moana Fisher
id. 9.102
b. 05.08.1976 Mornington, Vic
m.19.02.2000 Mornington, Vic

Leslie James Peck
id. 9.102A
b. 17.08.1973 Frankston, Vic

William Kelvin Tainui Fisher
id. 9.106
b. 28.02.1978 Mornington, Vic

Dennis Keith Pratt
id. 8.058
b. 04.05.1953
m.29.03.1975 Frankston, Vic

Robin Elizabeth Kennedy
id. 8.058A
b. 23.01.1957 Frankston, Vic

Benjamin William Pratt
id. 9.105
b. 06.07.1977 Frankston, Vic
m. 24.12.yyyy

Yvette Joy
id. 9.105A
b. 09.08.1976

Charlette Isabella Pratt
id. 10.130
b. 23.03.2005 Malvern, Vic

Lachlan Dennis Pratt
id. 10.140
b. 23.12.2006 Malvern, Vic

Timothy James Pratt
id. 9.109
b. 31.03.1981 Frankston, Vic

m. 15.11.1986 Bittern, Vic

Fiona Margaret Norton
id. 8.058B
b. 07.06.1957 Hawera, NZ

James Daniel Pratt
id. 9.114
b. 23. 07.1987 Frankston, Vic

APPENDIX 22

STATISTICS AND FACTS

1. A total of 438 descendants of the original Alexander Thom (id. 1.001) have been identified. Of those, approximately 71 per cent are living today.

2. All members of Generations 1 to 6 have passed on, and there is only one survivor of Generation 7; Mabel Pratt (née Hind, id. 7.042) of Australia; she was the last-born in that generation.

3. The numerically-dominant generation within the family is Generation 10, with 149 members currently; it most likely will continue to expand for some time.

4. Generation 11 commenced in 1995, so there is a reasonable probability that the following Generation 12 will start within the next 5 or so years. Births in Generation 11 probably will continue until about 2040.

5. The oldest male descendant to date has been Dillon Turner Thom (id. 6.014), who lived to eighty-nine years of age. The oldest female descendant to date has been Holly Budd (id. 7.023), who died aged eighty-eight. The oldest surviving

member is the above-mentioned Mabel Pratt, currently eighty-four years old.

6. The largest family to date has been that of Margaret Thom (id 5.001) and Frederick Pilkington, with eleven children.

7. The centre of gravity for the global family is now located in Australia, with about 68 per cent of the births in Generations 8-11 occurring there. Births in the United Kingdom and Ireland combined account for about 28 per cent, with the remaining 4 per cent shared around the globe.

8. Figure 34 summarises the statistics for the known global family population. It should be noted that with the exception of those sub-branches of the Pilkington branch where direct contact has been made, there is little information on the Pilkingtons beyond Generation 7. The inclusion of all such additional Pilkington descendants in all likelihood would materially affect the numbers shown here. It should also be noted that the statistics do not include the descendants, if any, of the siblings of either Alexander in Generation 2 or of Walter in Generation 3. If those family lines had produced at the same rate as the family lines covered in this book, the number of descendants of our original Alexander (id. 1.001) would be twelve times greater than that shown in Figure 34.

Generation No.	Male		Female		Total Members	First Birth	Last Birth	With Issue
	Dec'd	Living	Dec'd	Living				
1	1				1	1715	-	1
2	1		1		2	1738	1742	1*
3	4		2		6	1764	1773	1*
4	1		3		4	1801	1806	1
5	6		3		9	1825	1838	4
6	16		13		29	1845	1885	12
7	21		20	1	42	1868	1927	20
8	16	18	6	19	59	1910	1955	43
9	3	48	2	59	112	1941	1989	60
10	3	77	2	67	149	1966	2012	14
11		15		11	26	1995	2012	0
Total	72	158	52	157	439			

Figure 34: Statistics

* Siblings
not
researched.

INDEX

FAMILY DESCENDANTS

Blair	Maxwell	Thomson				10.131	227
Braun	Caroline					9.019	208
Braun	Nicholas					9.014	208
Brooks	Caroline	Elizabeth				9.086	214
Brooks	Gillian	Hazel				9.096	215
Brooks	Joanna	Hilary				9.112	215
Brooks	Leo	Ytang	Morcillo			10.156	215
Brooks	Robyn	Alejandra	Morcillo			10.147	215
Budd	Albert	Raymond				8.010	219
Budd	Brenda	Elaine				8.030	220
Budd	Charles	Thomas				8.009	219
Budd	Clova	Muriel	Daphne			8.011	219
Budd	Cullen	Hamlet				8.018	219
Budd	Earl	Lewin				8.021	219
Budd	Kathleen	Aileen	May			8.014	219
Budd	Nelson	Clarence				8.035	221
Budd	Silver	Merle	Lilian	Margaret		8.023	219
Budd	Trevor					9.012	219
Buha	Kate	Natalie				10.132	236
Buha	Luke	Nathan				10.144	236
Buha	Nathan	Josip				10.121	236
Burgess	Brooke	Veronica				10.048	220
Burgess	Gavin	James				9.035	220
Burgess	Jake	James				10.076	220
Burgess	Logan	John				10.035	219
Burgess	Peter	Anthony				9.030	220
Burgess	Reece	Desmond				10.062	220
Burgess	Robert	John				9.026	219
Burgess	Ryan	Daniel				10.031	219
Callaghan	Jackson	Leigh				10.084	221
Callaghan	Jessica	Rose				10.049	221
Callaghan	Scott	Christopher	Myles			10.060	221
Campion	Debbie	Jane				10.013	229
Campion	Michelle	Anne				10.004	229
Carrigan	Davis	Matthew				10.029	233
Chessum	Chelsea	Anne				11.021	222
Clarisse	Bailey	Jacob				10.103	234
Clarisse	Holly	Rose				10.113	234
Clarisse	Rubie	Mae				10.122	235
Coffey	Alison	Rosemary				9.094	214
Coffey	Clare	Wilha				9.076	214
de la Flor	Daniel					10.009	206
de la Flor	David					10.003	206

Henderson	Blake				10.065	223
Henderson	Brian	Clarence			8.043	223
Henderson	Clarence	Thomas	Robert	William	7.024	221
Henderson	Clarence				8.022	221
Henderson	Colette	Belle			10.153	211
Henderson	Craig	Brian			9.101	223
Henderson	Dana	Siobhan			9.110	211
Henderson	David				10.044	223
Henderson	Hazel	Sarah			8.052	211
Henderson	Holly	Lavinia	Eileen		7.023	219
Henderson	Joanne				9.063	223
Henderson	John	Watson	Reid		8.050	211
Henderson	Kurt				10.086	223
Henderson	Lucy				8.033	223
Henderson	Mara	Jane			9.100	211
Henderson	Margaret	Jessie	Iris		8.029	221
Henderson	Nelson	James	Albert		7.030	223
Henderson	Paul	William			9.055	223
Henderson	Shan	William			9.090	211
Henderson	Trucie	Sarah			9.080	211
Higgins	Gareth	Leslie			10.073	221
Higgins	Leonard	John			10.061	221
Hind	Aaron				10.101	232
Hind	Aaron	Helmut			10.087	234
Hind	Alexander	Joseph	James		7.029	229
Hind	Bessie	Mabel	Kathleen		7.041	235
Hind	Carol	Anne			8.051	234
Hind	Cassandra	Elizabeth			10.069	232
Hind	Catherine	Annette			9.027	230
Hind	Cheryl	Robin			9.020	229
Hind	Colin	Joseph	Claridge		8.059	235
Hind	David	James			9.047	232
Hind	Emilee				10.090	231
Hind	Emily	Veronica			10.129	234
Hind	Eva	Victoria	Dillon		7.037	233
Hind	Greer	Louise			10.037	231
Hind	Hayden	Mark			10.099	234
Hind	Heath	Andrew			9.111	235
Hind	Isabel	Mabel	Elizabeth		7.033	229
Hind	James	Henry			8.031	232
Hind	James	Thomas			7.039	234
Hind	James	Wade			10.041	231
Hind	Jamie	Christopher			10.107	234

Hind	Jamie	Robert		9.069	232
Hind	Janice	Gay		9.023	230
Hind	Jayden			10.054	231
Hind	Jessica	Elizabeth		10.118	234
Hind	John	Charles		9.064	231
Hind	John	Henry		8.057	234
Hind	Justin			10.115	232
Hind	Kaiden	Matthew		11.022	231
Hind	Kelly	Anne		9.093	232
Hind	Lachlan			10.080	231
Hind	Lee	Stephen		10.042	231
Hind	Leslie	James		9.097	234
Hind	Mabel	Marjory		7.042	236
Hind	Mark	Henry		9.061	232
Hind	Matthew	Dean		10.045	231
Hind	Matthew	John		9.099	235
Hind	Michelle	Anne		9.107	234
Hind	Neville	Alexander		8.024	229
Hind	Nicholas			10.066	231
Hind	Norman	James	William	8.055	234
Hind	Pamela	Gay		8.044	232
Hind	Peter	James		10.057	232
Hind	Peter	Thomas		10.053	231
Hind	Raymond	James		9.040	231
Hind	Rebecca			10.091	232
Hind	Riley	William		10.149	234
Hind	Robert	Claridge		7.035	229
Hind	Robert	Claridge		8.025	229
Hind	Robert	Terence		10.033	231
Hind	Robert	William		9.034	230
Hind	Sarah	Louise		10.083	232
Hind	Stacey			10.117	232
Hind	Tracey	Lee		9.084	234
Hind	Valerie	June		8.026	231
Hind	Zachary	James		10.137	234
Hornidge	Aileen	Felicity		9.006	207
Hornidge	Brian	Guy		8.015	208
Hornidge	Carol	Heather		9.010	206
Hornidge	Christopher	Rowan		9.004	208
Hornidge	Deirdre	Lidderdale		9.003	207
Hornidge	Denis	Richard		8.007	206
Hornidge	Dudley	George	Pilkington	7.012	206
Hornidge	Gail	Priscilla		9.016	206

Hornidge	Gillian	Rona			9.033	206
Hornidge	Guy	Mulock	Pilkington		7.015	207
Hornidge	Jennifer	Francis	Lilias		9.015	207
Hornidge	John	Dudley			8.001	206
Hornidge	Olive	Hilda	Beatrice	Pilkington	7.008	205
Hornidge	Pamela	Marjery			8.005	206
Hornidge	Patrick	Rowan			8.002	207
Hornidge	Sheilagh	Mary			8.017	208
Hornidge	Susan	Lorraine			9.007	206
Hornidge	Sybil	Pilkington			7.004	205
Hornidge	Vanessa				9.002	208
Hornidge	Veronica	Geraldine			9.001	208
Hughes	William	John			10.098	226
Hughes	Winston	Thom	Raymond		10.109	226
Jacobs	Brylie	Leah			10.040	222
Jacobs	Rhys	Dylan			10.067	222
Jacobs	Teoni	Ellen			10.047	222
Jenner	Edward				10.025	206
Jenner	Thomas	Robert			10.015	206
Jeudwine	XXX	(male)			8.003	209
Kneebone	Caitlyn	Louise			11.012	220
Kneebone	Cheryl	Elaine			9.059	221
Kneebone	Daniel	Nathan			10.050	221
Kneebone	James				11.024	220
Kneebone	Joshua	David			10.088	221
Kneebone	Kayden				11.013	220
Kneebone	Kristy	Peta			10.027	220
Kneebone	Matthew	Norman			10.022	220
Kneebone	Peter	Norman			9.029	220
Kneebone	Shannon	Rebecca			10.070	221
Kneebone	Stephen	Leslie			9.041	220
Kneebone	Tamara	Jade			10.036	221
Kneebone	Tracy	Lee			10.023	220
Knight	Colin	Alexander	Robert		8.019	229
Knight	Peter	Anthony			9.053	229
Knowler	James	Robin			10.010	207
Knowler	Meredith	Jane			10.005	207
Kuffer	Aaron	Jason			10.014	231
Kuffer	Michelle	Deanne			10.011	231
Long	Darcy	Jackson			10.064	222
Long	Dylan	Brodie			10.074	222
Long	Jarrod	Tyler			10.051	222
Long	Thomas	Ryan			10.038	222

Pilkington	Frederick	Ernest	Chomley	7.005	208
Pilkington	Frederick	Mervyn	Fosbery	7.019	208
Pilkington	Hamlet	Wade		6.007	208
Pilkington	Joyce	Eileen		8.006	205
Pilkington	Lionel			7.010	205
Pilkington	Lyulph	Frederick		7.013	205
Pilkington	Margaret	Elizabeth		6.001	205
Pilkington	Maria			6.005	208
Pilkington	Mina	Olive		7.007	208
Pilkington	Olivia	Wade		6.006	208
Pilkington	Violet	Josephine		6.011	209
Pilkington	William	Handcock		6.008	208
Plastow	Beverley	Joy		8.048	235
Plastow	Edwin	James		8.053	236
Plastow	Lorraine	Joy		8.046	235
Plastow	Sally	Elizabeth		9.104	236
Plastow	Zoe	Margaret		9.115	236
Powell	Alan			8.049	233
Powell	Anthony	John		9.087	233
Powell	Bronwyn	Denise		9.068	233
Powell	Carl	Henry		9.058	233
Powell	Geoffrey	James		9.074	233
Powell	Henry			8.041	233
Powell	James	Henry		8.034	233
Powell	Katherine	Louise		9.071	233
Powell	Micah	James		9.067	233
Powell	Narelle	Louise		9.092	233
Powell	Robert			8.054	233
Powell	Shane	Robert		9.103	233
Powell	Stephen	David		9.113	233
Pratt	Benjamin	William		9.105	236
Pratt	Charlette	Isabella		10.130	236
Pratt	Christine	Janice		8.056	236
Pratt	Dennis	Keith		8.058	236
Pratt	James	Daniel		9.114	237
Pratt	Lachlan	Dennis		10.140	236
Pratt	Timothy	James		9.109	237
Richards	Caitlin	Elouise		10.055	230
Richards	Patrick	Charles		10.077	230
Ritchie	Anya	Minnie	Elizabeth	10.126	214
Ritchie	Ronan	Ed	Mossie	10.138	214
Ritchie	Sian	Hilary	Rebecca	10.150	214
Schwarz	Adam	James		10.114	225

Schwarz	Benjamin	Robert			10.081	225
Schwarz	Emily	Jean			10.097	225
Spencer	Emma				9.098	211
Spencer	Helen	Elizabeth	Sarah		9.108	211
Stephens	Belinda				10.020	206
Stephens	Catherine	Alexandra			10.017	206
Studley	Brianna	Jane			10.120	232
Studley	Jordyn	Leigh			10.108	232
Sword	James	Robert	William		10.032	217
Sword	Juliet	Vanessa			10.056	217
Sword	Marie	Louise			9.021	217
Sword	Rupert	Robert			9.017	217
Thom	Albert	Charles	Alexander	Robert	6.026	203
Thom	Albert	Edward			7.036	226
Thom	Alexander				1.001	202
Thom	Alexander				2.002	202
Thom	Alexander				3.002	202
Thom	Alexander				4.001	202
Thom	Alexander				5.005	203
Thom	Alexander				6.012	211
Thom	Alexander	Edward	Dillon		9.042	217
Thom	Alexander	Seward	Dillon		7.028	212
Thom	Alice	Margaret	Kathleen	Eva	6.022	203
Thom	Anne				2.001	202
Thom	Barbara	Dillon			8.036	213
Thom	Bolton	Dillon			7.031	212
Thom	Brian	Geoffrey			8.028	225
Thom	Carolyn	Faye			8.047	226
Thom	Catherine	Jean			9.057	225
Thom	Christian				3.001	202
Thom	Colin	William			8.037	226
Thom	Daphne	Evelyn	Patricia		8.020	217
Thom	Darryl	Ernest			8.039	226
Thom	Dillon	Turner			6.014	212
Thom	Elizabeth	Helen			4.002	203
Thom	Elizabeth	Helen			4.003	203
Thom	Fanny	Alberta	Cora	Jane	6.024	203, 219
Thom	Fraser	Colin	McGregor		9.070	226
Thom	Frederick	Pilkington			6.021	215
Thom	Frederick	Robert			6.025	215
Thom	Geoffrey	Walter			7.034	225
Thom	Gladys	Lilian			7.032	225
Thom	Graeme	Edward			8.032	226

Thom	Henry	Bentley			7.025	212
Thom	Henry	Edward	Dillon		8.013	217
Thom	Hilary	Doris			8.045	214
Thom	Hubert	Ernest			6.023	215
Thom	James				3.004	202
Thom	Jean				3.006	203
Thom	Jean				4.004	203
Thom	John				3.003	202
Thom	John	Bolton	Ruxton		6.020	215
Thom	Lisa	Jane			9.072	225
Thom	Lucy	Elizabeth			10.072	225
Thom	Mabel	Beatrice	Louisa	Jane	6.029	203, 229
Thom	Margaret				5.001	202, 205
Thom	Margaret	Evelyn			8.027	212
Thom	Maria				5.006	203
Thom	Maria	Victoria	Elizabeth		6.016	215
Thom	Megan	Joanne			9.078	226
Thom	Melinda	Elizabeth			9.077	226
Thom	Monica	Patricia			9.038	217
Thom	Noel	Lindsay			8.038	226
Thom	Patrick				5.003	202
Thom	Robert				5.004	202
Thom	Robert				5.008	203
Thom	Robert				6.017	215
Thom	Rosemary	Constance			8.040	214
Thom	Sally	Elizabeth			9.043	225
Thom	Sarah				6.018	215
Thom	Sarah	Kristen			9.091	226
Thom	Sarah	Watson			7.040	211
Thom	Sidney	Frances	Thornburgh		6.015	202
Thom	Susan	Louise			9.050	225
Thom	Susan	Louise			9.085	227
Thom	Sylvia	Daphne			9.051	217
Thom	Victoria	Jane			5.009	203
Thom	Victoria	Maria	Annie	Dillon	6.019	203
Thom	Walter				3.005	202
Thom	Walter				5.002	202
Thom	Walter				5.007	203, 2011
Thom	Walter				6.013	212
Thom	Walter	Dillon			7.027	212, 217
Thom	William	Nathaniel	Walter	Hamlet	6.027	203
Thom	William	Nathaniel	Walter	Hamlet	6.028	203, 225
Turbett	Glenda	Karen			9.088	235

Turbett	Paul	Steven		9.075	235
Turk	Aileen	Besire		11.015	207
Wain	Brayden	Kevin		10.119	235
Wain	Cooper	Richard		10.154	235
Wain	David	Kevin		9.073	235
Wain	Julie	Joy		9.079	235
Wain	Lachlan	Flynn		10.139	235
Ware	Brenton	James		11.002	229
Ware	Jacob	Francis		11.001	229
Williams	Andrew	Norman		9.022	219
Williams	Michael	Anthony		9.031	219
Wood	Alasdair	Keith		10.110	213
Wood	Georgia	Grace		10.116	213
Wyper	Lauren	Hornidge		10.030	207
Wyper	Siobhan	Lilias		10.019	207

FAMILY NON-DESCENDANTS

Family Name	1st Given	2nd Given	3rd Given	4th Given	ID. No.	Page
Abela	Margaret	Mary			8.055 B	234
Adams	Craig	Robert			9.088 B	235
Albiol	Ytang	Morcillo			9.112 A	215
Allen	Eric	George			9.027 A	230
Allen	Gregory	Bruce			9.023 A	230
Atkinson	Ronald	Leslie			8.029 A	221
Awty	Pauline	Margaret			8.053 A	236
Bahl	Ashlee	Maree			10.043 A	231
Barrett	Michael	Robert	Lambart		8.036 A	213
Bemelmans	Joseph	Matthew			8.044 A	232
Berry	Iris	Elsie			7.024 A	221
Berry	James				7.008 B	205
Bjorlin	Carlos	Edwin			8.005 A	206
Blair	Christopher	Stuart			9.085 B	227
Blair	Helen	Lorraine	Steel		8.001 A	206
Blair	Jordan	Sebastian	James		10.078	227
Blair	Niall	Ambrose			10.085	227
Blewitt	Cheryl	Anne			9.055 A	223
Bolton	Mary	Ann	Ruxton		5.007 A	211
Braun	Martin				8.017 A	208
Brooks	Maurice	John			8.045 A	214
Browne	Sidney	Thornburgh			5.003 A	202
Bryan	Bertha	Charlotte	Georgina		7.019 A	208
Budd	Thomas				7.023 A	219
Buha	Michael	James			9.079 A	235
Bundle	Michael	David			9.088 A	235
Burgess	Brian	Daniel			8.023 A	219
Burgess	Karen	Lynette			9.083	220
Callaghan	Christopher				9.059 A	221
Cameron	Muriel	Sylvia			8.019 A	229
Campbell	James				7.008 A	205
Campion	Stephen				9.020 A	229

Carrigan	Gregory	Peter		9.048 A	232
Casey	Donna			9.045 A	222
Cheng	Longyi			10.043	219
Cheng	Xiao	Hue		9.031 A	219
Chessum	Russell	John		10.028 A	222
Chisholm	Belinda	Jane		9.073 A	235
Chuck	Wattie			7.038 C	223
Clarisse	Mark	Tracy		9.084 A	234
Clutton	Marnie	Elizabeth		9.047 A	232
Coffey	Robert	Hugh	Ivan	8.040 A	214
Cook	Vera	Edith		7.029 A	229
Cortous	Doris	May		7.034 A	225
Coutts	Pamela			8.034 B	233
Cox	Annie			5.008 A	203
Cravino	Beryl	May		7.036 A	226
Crothall	Shirley	Anne		8.037 A	226
Cusack	Ralph	Smith	Oliver	7.006 A	205
Dawson	Millicent	Lilias	Yelverton	8.007 A	206
d'Bentley	Mary	Evelyn		6.014 A	212
de la Flor	Carlos			9.010 A	206
de Smit	Paul			8.047 B	226
Delphin	Geoffrey	Ian		10.023 A	220
Denton	Donald	MacLean		8.027 A	212
Dezaayer	Yvonne			9.032 A	221
Dillon	Maria			4.001 A	202
Dixon	Nicolette			9.029 A	220
Dorward	Margaret			1.001 A	202
Elling	David			9.010 B	206
Estcourt	XXX			9.093 A	232
Farhoud	Issa			9.046 A	213
Finch	Diane	Raylene		9.041 A	220
Fisher	Kelvin	Wiremu		8.056 A	236
Foster	Ryan	Steven		9.096 A	215
Fowler	Eric			7.038 A	223
Friend	Adam	John		9.104 A	236
Fulton	Thomas			10.002 A	207
Ginger	Carl			9.100 A	211

Glasson	Darren	Ross		9.083 A	220
Glasson	Natasha	Zoe		10.104	220
Glasson	Victoria	Rose		10.151	220
Goff	Jessie	Elizabeth		7.039 A	234
Gonzales	Jorge	Mata		10.019 A	207
Goodes	Justin	Andrew		9.078 A	226
Gorman	Andrew	Roger		9.076 A	214
Gorman	Wilhelmina	Margaret		7.031 A	212
Gray	Elizabeth			6.026 A	203
Gregg	Huband.	George		6.011 A	209
Gregg	Timothy	Charles	William	9.011	209
Hall	John			7.002 B	205
Hall	Phyllis	Anne		7.029 B	229
Halliday	Neil			10.030 A	207
Hanson	June			8.059 B	235
Harden	Kathleen	Anne		7.012 A	206
Hartrick	Karen			9.032 B	221
Harvey	Jodie	Danielle		9.082	226
Harvey	John	Desmond		8.047 A	226
Henderson	Christian			2.002 A	202
Henderson	Frank			7.038 B	223
Henderson	Herbert	John	Reid	7.040 A	211
Henderson	William	John		6.024 A	219
Higgins	David	Brian		9.028 A	221
Hind	James	Henry	Claridge	6.029 A	229
Honey	Joanne	Margaret		9.035 A	220
Hookings	Jilliene	Rae		8.028 A	225
Horne	Frederick	Alexander		9.050 A	225
Hornidge	John			6.003 A	205
Howrit	Nancy	May		8.009 A	219
Hughes	Steven	John		9.077 A	226
Humphrey	Christine			8.031 A	232
Hutchinson	Glenda			9.030 B	220
Jacobs	Garry	John		9.049 A	222
Jenner	John	Richard		9.016 A	206
Jeudwine	Richard	William	Rice	7.022 A	209
Johnson	Caroline	Audrey		9.089 A	226

Joy	Yvette			9.105 A	236
Kennedy	Robin	Elizabeth		8.058 A	236
Key	XXX	(Spencer)		9.098 A	211
King	Daphne			7.027 A	217
Kingsland	Ivy	May		7.035 A	229
Kneebone	Clarence	Norman		8.030 A	220
Knight	George	Crawford		7.033 A	229
Knowler	David	John		9.003 A	207
Kuffer	Kurt			9.025 A	231
Langley	Carol	Anne		8.055 A	234
Lerault	Laurence	France		9.044 A	212
Logan	Joanne	Karen		9.075 A	235
Long	Jackson			9.054 A	222
Lyons	John	Charles		6.010 A	209
Mackay	Sarah			4.001 B	202
Mackay	William	Lindsay		5.010	202
Maguire	Glenn	Douglas		10.013 A	229
Marshall	Colin	James		9.072 A	225
Matarazzo	Carlos	Alberto		9.021 A	217
Matthews	Joan	Wilma		8.043 A	223
Maunsell	Caroline	Rhys	Robertson	7.028 B	212
Mayhew	Agnes			6.002 A	205
Mayne	Robert	St John		6.001 A	205
Mc Fadden	Keith			8.023 B	219
McConnell	David	Edgar		9.056 A	214
McCormack	Bree	Louise		10.008 A	230
McDonald	Valerie			8.053 B	236
McKenzie	Kenneth	Mervyn		8.051 A	234
McKenzie	Sarah	Elaynah		10.018 A	230
McKie	Brian			8.026 A	231
McLean	Maureen			8.039 A	226
McLean	Trevor			9.063 A	223
McNamara	Daniel	Jay		10.024 A	222
McNiffe	Anne	Marie		9.024 A	221
Meggs	Karen			8.059 A	235
Melo	Oscar	Spinoza		9.021 B	217
Mentzel	Hannelore			9.018 A	206

Mitchell	Edward	Anthony	Julian	Simon	9.080 A	211
Murphy	Sarah	Paine			6.012 A	211
Needham	Bryan	Donald			9.006 A	207
Norton	Fiona	Margaret			8.058 B	237
Ogilvy	John	Augustine			8.008 A	209
Olesker	Carolina	Mintz			10.007 A	217
O'Neill	Sharon	Leigh			9.041 B	220
Ormond	Mark	John			10.026 A	207
Ormsby	John	Arthur	Cooper		6.001 B	205
Overmars	Kathleen	Patricia			8.025 A	229
Oxenford	Ursula	Marian			7.019 B	208
Pearce	Brian				9.037 A	231
Pearson	Flora				7.015 A	207
Peatling	Deborah	May			9.030 A	220
Peck	Leslie	James			9.102 A	236
Pemberton	Andrew	Carl			9.095 A	236
Pike	Joan	Ellen			8.054 A	233
Pike	Lucinda				6.028 B	225
Pilkington	Frederick				5.001 A	205
Pilson	Arthur	Forde			7.001 A	205
Plant	Fay				8.010 A	219
Plastow	Richard	Frederick			7.041 A	235
Potter	Lilian				6.028 A	225
Powell	Henry	Albert	Alexander		7.037 A	233
Pratt	William	James			7.042 A	236
Prescott	Beverley				8.004 A	209
Ramadge	Smith	Ramadge			7.002 A	205
Rankin	Patricia	Ann			8.038 A	226
Reynolds	Denise	Eleanor			8.024 A	229
Richards	Beverley	Anne			9.036 A	222
Richards	Neville	James			9.027 B	230
Richardson	Kathleen				6.008 A	208
Rienierts	Louise	Maria			9.034 A	230
Ritchie	Paul	Edgar			9.086 A	214
Robb	Alvis				8.007 B	206
Roberts	Elwyn	Joy			8.028 B	225
Row	Raymond	Reginald	Holt		9.043 A	225

Russell	Evelyn	Constance		6.014 B	212
Rynd	Scrope	Bernard	Christopher	6.006 A	208
Saddlier	Kay	Lynette		9.026 A	219
Sandhu	Sarbjit	Kaur		10.015 A	206
Santos	Angela	Inez		8.002 A	207
Schahinger	Robert	Wayne		9.003 B	207
Schreffler	Florence	Mae		7.021 A	209
Schreiner	Frances	Lyndall		7.017 A	209
Schukraft	Norma	Anne		8.034 A	233
Schwarz	Peter	Craig		9.057 A	225
Sheezel	Julian	Marcus		9.085 A	227
Skrine	Ralph	Hanham		7.022 B	209
Soitel	Bertrand	Jean	Francois	10.089	212
Soitel	Julien	Georges	Henri	10.079	212
Sparks	Beatrice	Thirza		7.015 A	208
Spencer	Richard	Andrew		8.052 A	211
Stephens	Bertha	Harriet	Maud	7.010 A	205
Stephens	Michael	Alexander		9.007 A	206
Strachan	Leonie			9.069 A	232
Stray	Heath	Richard		10.024 B	222
Studley	Christopher	Leigh		9.093 B	232
Summerill	Jane	Elspeth		9.017 A	217
Sword	Robert	Weare		8.020 A	217
Sylvester	Tamzin			9.090 A	211
Taylor	Susan	Jane		8.042 A	211
Terry	Lorraine			8.041 A	233
Tobin	Kerri	Elizabeth		8.057 A	234
Turbett	David	George		8.046 A	235
Turk	Ozcan			10.001 A	207
Turner	Margaret			3.005 A	202
Urbancic	Stephanie			9.030 C	220
Vargas	Aurora	Del Carmen		8.013 A	217
Wade	Susan	Louise		9.040 A	231
Wain	Kevin	John		8.048 A	235
Ware	John	Francis		10.004 A	229
West	Vanessa	Jane		9.070 A	226
Whittington	Alison	Jane		9.039 A	213

Wilkes	Malcolm			9.033 B	206
Williams	Jack	Desmond		10.141	226
Williams	Jeffrey	Joseph		9.082 A	226
Williams	Reginald	Alfred		8.014 A	219
Wilson	Margaret	Louisa		6.004 A	208
Wonfor	Susanne			9.062 A	213
Wood	Richard	James		9.052 A	213
Woodwright	William	Henry	Edward	7.003 A	205
Wright	Doris	Hilary		7.028 A	212
Wyper	John	Campbell		9.015 A	207
XXX	Rebecca	(Hind)		9.064 A	231
XXX	Sheila	(Hornidge)		8.002 B	208
XXX	Simon	(Hornidge)		9.033 A	206
Zytek	Michelle	Louise		9.097 A	234

Lightning Source UK Ltd.
Milton Keynes UK
UKOW040213160513

210747UK00002B/97/P